CHER HAMPTON

Abandonment Recovery Handbook

Embracing the 5 Stages of Healing from Abandonment, Loss, and Heartbreak for Emotional Resilience and Grief Recovery

First published by Fidna Publishing 2023

Copyright © 2023 by Cher Hampton

All rights reserved. No part of this publication may be reproduced, stored or transmitted in any form or by any means, electronic, mechanical, photocopying, recording, scanning, or otherwise without written permission from the publisher. It is illegal to copy this book, post it to a website, or distribute it by any other means without permission.

Under no circumstances will any blame or legal responsibility be held against the publisher, or author, for any damages, reparation, or monetary loss due to the information contained within this book, either directly or indirectly.

Disclaimer Notice:

Please note the information contained within this document is for educational and entertainment purposes only. All effort has been executed to present accurate, up to date, reliable, complete information. No warranties of any kind are declared or implied. Readers acknowledge that the author is not engaged in the rendering of legal, financial, medical or professional advice. The content within this book has been derived from various sources. Please consult a licensed professional before attempting any techniques outlined in this book.

By reading this document, the reader agrees that under no circumstances is the author responsible for any losses, direct or indirect, that are incurred as a result of the use of the information contained within this document, including, but not limited to, errors, omissions, or inaccuracies.

First edition

*This book was professionally typeset on Reedsy.
Find out more at reedsy.com*

Contents

Introduction	iv
1 Understanding Abandonment, Loss, and Heartbreak	1
2 Navigating Abandonment Issues	12
3 The Five Stages of Abandonment Healing	26
4 Embracing Denial and Acceptance	39
5 Transforming Anger and Bargaining	51
6 Navigating the Depths of Depression	66
7 Finding Healing in Acceptance	80
8 Building Emotional Resilience Beyond Healing	99
9 Make Your Own Action Plan	110
10 Extra Exercises to Recover From Abandonment	116
Bonus: Your Free Gifts	128
Conclusion	130
References	133

Introduction

"The wound is the place where the light enters you."

— Rumi

Welcome to this voyage, fellow travelers, on the path to healing. If you're holding this book, you've embarked on a journey to navigate the tempestuous waters of abandonment, loss, and heartbreak, with the promise of emerging stronger, and more resilient. I'm Cher Hampton, and I'm here to be your guide and confidant on this transformative voyage.

Have you ever felt the weight of emotions dragging you down? The gnawing ache of abandonment, the piercing grief of loss, the raw ache of heartbreak—these emotions can seem insurmountable. You may feel alone, but you've felt these struggles as every other human being. And it's precisely from these battles that you can harness your strength to rise above, to forge emotional resilience that can withstand life's storms.

Imagine a life where your wounds become your sources of power, your scars symbols of resilience. This is the journey I invite you to embark on as you open this book—an expedition that leads you from the depths of pain to the heights of emotional strength.

But why trust me to take you on this journey? Because I've walked this path. I've navigated the labyrinthine corridors of abandonment and faced the echoing silence of loss. These personal experiences, intertwined with my academic and professional background, have led me to a mission: to guide individuals like you through the process of healing and resilience.

Growing up, I learned life's lessons earlier than most. The dissolution of my parents' relationship and the tragic loss of a close loved one shaped my formative years. The aftermath of these events left me grappling with abandonment issues, a shadow that would linger for years. But rather than succumbing to despair, I chose to transform my pain into purpose.

Fueled by a burning desire to not only heal myself but to help others navigate their own struggles, I pursued a path in psychology. This path, paired with my personal experiences, equipped me with a unique perspective to lead you through the stages of healing.

So, what lies ahead in this book? Practical guidance. No platitudes or empty promises. Each chapter is a guide through the intricacies of healing—from understanding the stages of denial, anger, bargaining, depression, and acceptance, to embracing strategies that foster emotional resilience. We'll dive into the heart of each stage, utilizing critical thinking, scientific evidence, and empathy to light our way.

Are you ready to embark on this journey? To transform your pain into strength and your struggles into tools for growth? If so, join me as we take that first step together. Let's uncover the stages of healing, nurture emotional resilience, and embrace the transformation that awaits.

Turn the page, your travel toward emotional resilience begins now.

1

Understanding Abandonment, Loss, and Heartbreak

"The loss of a loved one is one of the most profound experiences of human existence."

— John Bowlby

In this chapter, we start by embarking on a profound exploration of abandonment, loss, and heartbreak, those intricate emotions that can redefine our very existence.

Consider for a moment the deep well of pain that accompanies the loss of a loved one, the lingering ache of abandonment, or the shattering impact of heartbreak. These experiences possess the power to leave us adrift in an ocean of emotions, causing us to mourn not only the absence of a person but also the death of our expectations, hopes, and dreams. The emotions we associate with abandonment or the lack of love can be likened to a process of mourning, not just for what once was, but for the illusions we held.

There is a profound and intricate parallel that runs between heartbreak and the sorrow of losing someone to death. This connection is not based on a vast body of research that has meticulously analyzed the psychological underpinnings of these experiences.

In the realm of psychology, researchers have unveiled the intricate ways in which our brains process heartbreak and the loss of a loved one—all of them types of abandonment. When we experience heartbreak, the emotional pain registers in the same regions of the brain that are activated when we lose a cherished person to death. This overlap of neural pathways reflects the universality of human emotions, suggesting that whether the source of pain is a physical absence or emotional disconnection, our brains process these experiences with a remarkable degree of similarity (Tamam & Ahmad, 2017).

The emotional rollercoaster that accompanies abandonment, heartbreak, and loss is underscored by the activation of the brain's reward centers, which are involved in pleasurable experiences like love and attachment. When these attachments are severed, whether through the dissolution of a relationship or the finality of death, the brain experiences an acute sense of loss that triggers a cascade of emotional responses. This is where the concept of anguish and longing comes into play; two emotions that are strikingly comparable between the two scenarios.

On the other hand, our physiological responses also emphasize the connection between heartbreak and loss. During times of intense emotional distress, our bodies release stress hormones such as cortisol and adrenaline. These hormones prepare us to react to threats, but in the context of emotional pain, they can lead to a heightened state of anxiety, restlessness, and even physical discomfort. Research has shown that these physiological responses are remarkably consistent, whether we're grappling with heartbreak or mourning a departed loved one (Tamam & Ahmad, 2017).

In essence, the human experience of abandonment, heartbreak, and loss reveals a profound truth: Our emotions transcend the boundaries of circumstance. Whether it's the death of a cherished individual or the dissolution of an emotional bond, the human psyche navigates these experiences with similar mechanisms.

As I recollect my early adolescence, a personal experience stands out; one occasion that introduced me to the profound pain of heartbreak. It was a connection severed, a love unreturned. The agony was all-encompassing, a weight pressing on my chest that made each breath an effort. Perhaps you, too, can recall a moment when the end of a relationship or the fading of a connection felt like an emotional earthquake, rendering the world unfamiliar and leaving you to grapple with the aftershocks. Such pain isn't confined to a specific age, gender, or culture; it's a universal thread that weaves through the human experience.

In those moments of heartbreak, it feels as if the world ceases to move, as if the universe holds its breath in anticipation of our grief. Unamuno's words capture this sentiment: For us, it feels like the universe has stopped; for the world, it continues its relentless march forward.

As we journey through this chapter, our aim is not merely to skim the surface of these emotions; it's to dissect them with both scientific rigor and empathetic insight. We're peering beneath the surface of abandonment, loss, and heartbreak to understand their multifaceted nature.

Let's start by shedding light on the complex jumble of emotions that we'll be navigating through in this chapter. According to the Merriam-Webster (n.d.) dictionary, abandonment refers to the act of leaving something or someone behind, often associated with feelings of desertion or neglect. Loss is defined as the process of losing something or someone, resulting in a state of bereavement or deprivation. Heartbreak is described as intense emotional suffering or distress caused by a painful experience, particularly the end of a relationship or the loss of a loved one.

But let's venture beyond mere dictionary definitions and delve into the profound human experiences that these terms encapsulate. Abandonment isn't just about physical departure; it's the feeling of being left adrift, emotionally stranded, and grappling with a void that aches to be filled.

In the attachment theory developed by John Bowlby (1969), abandonment is seen as the disruption or loss of a secure emotional bond, typically between a child and their primary caregiver. It encompasses feelings of rejection, isolation, and fear of being unloved or unwanted. Abandonment can also extend to adulthood, where it manifests as the fear of rejection in personal relationships, often leading to clinginess, jealousy, or emotional withdrawal.

Loss isn't confined to possessions; it's the profound sense of emptiness that takes root when something dear to us is no longer present. It encompasses not only the loss of relationships but also the loss of cherished possessions, opportunities, or even aspects of oneself, such as health or identity. It is related to the stages of grief outlined in the Kübler-Ross model (Tyrrell et al., 2023): denial, anger, bargaining, depression, and acceptance.

And heartbreak, well, it's not just the shattering of romantic notions; it's the visceral pain that permeates our being when the connections we held dear crumble. It's akin to the stages of grief in the Kübler-Ross model, particularly the stages of anger and depression, as individuals grapple with the emotional turmoil of a severed bond.

The nuances between these emotions are subtle yet significant. Abandonment is closely linked to feelings of rejection and fear of being unloved, often stemming from early attachment experiences. It can stem from a feeling of being overlooked or unvalued, even if the source isn't a physical departure. You can feel abandoned by a partner you sleep in the same bed with.

Loss encompasses a broader spectrum, including the grief experienced when something dear to us is no longer present, it's about the absence of something cherished, whether it's a loved one, a relationship, or a prized possession. The most illustrative example is probably when a loved one passes away. Heartbreak, while intimately connected to love, extends to any profound emotional connection we have with others.

A broken heart can be the cause of a break in an affective relationship, even a non-romantic one, where the ties we have woven are broken, leaving us emotionally devastated. The betrayal of a family member or friend, for example, can destroy us as much as a love breakup.

However, these emotions also transcend cultural boundaries, albeit with variations in perception and expression. In some cultures, abandonment may be perceived as a loss of face or honor, leading to intense shame. In others, it might manifest as a deep sense of communal responsibility (Kramer et al., 2002).

Consider a traditional family in many East Asian cultures, where maintaining family honor and reputation is of paramount importance. In such a culture, a young adult who decides to move away from their family to pursue a career opportunity in a distant city might be seen as abandoning their familial responsibilities. This action could bring intense shame to the family, as it may be perceived as a breach of duty and an abandonment of traditions. The family may feel that their honor is tarnished due to this perceived abandonment.

Now, imagine a close-knit indigenous community in a remote part of the world. In this community, everyone plays a crucial role in maintaining their way of life. If a member of this community decides to leave for an extended period, perhaps to pursue higher education or work in a distant city, the community might perceive this as abandonment. However, instead of shame, their response may be rooted in a deep sense of communal responsibility. They understand that the individual's departure is a necessary step for the betterment of the community as a whole, and they support this decision while also acknowledging the challenges it poses.

In these two contrasting examples, we see how the perception of abandonment varies based on cultural values and norms.

Similarly, loss can be met with mourning rituals or celebrations of life, reflecting cultural beliefs about the continuity of existence beyond death.

In Mexican culture, the concept of loss is often met with a unique and vibrant approach that combines mourning with celebrations of life. This perspective is deeply rooted in cultural beliefs that emphasize the continuity of existence beyond death.

One of the most prominent examples of this cultural outlook is the Dia de los Muertos, or Day of the Dead, a widely celebrated holiday in Mexico. During this event, families come together to remember and honor their loved ones who have passed away. While it might seem like a solemn occasion, it is, in fact, a joyful celebration of life's continuity.

Families create elaborate altars, known as ofrendas, adorned with marigold flowers, sugar skulls, candles, and the favorite foods and possessions of the departed. These ofrendas are meant to welcome the spirits of the deceased back to the world of the living. It's a time for families to reminisce about their loved ones, sharing stories and anecdotes, and feeling their presence among them.

In Mexican culture, death is seen not as an end but as a natural part of the human journey. It's believed that the spirits of the departed return during Dia de los Muertos to enjoy the offerings and the company of their living relatives. This belief in the continuity of existence beyond death shapes the way loss is experienced and expressed.

This unique approach to loss reflects a deep-seated cultural belief in celebrating life, even in the face of death. It emphasizes the idea that our loved ones live on in our memories and that death is not the final chapter. Instead, it's a transition to another form of existence, where they can still be a part of our lives and celebrations.

Heartbreak, on its side, has been historically expressed through artistic forms or stoicism, depending on the cultural context. Let's take Japanese culture as an example of this. Waka, a traditional Japanese poetic form, has been a channel for expressing deep emotions, including the pain of heartbreak.

Waka poets often composed verses that conveyed the profound sense of loss and longing that accompanies heartbreak. These poems, known as "tanka," are concise yet emotionally charged. They capture the fleeting beauty of love and the melancholy of its loss. This artistic expression provides an outlet for individuals to articulate their innermost feelings of heartbreak with elegance and precision (Encyclopædia Britannica, n.d.).

In contrast, certain cultural contexts, such as traditional British culture, have historically emphasized stoicism in the face of heartbreak. The "stiff upper lip" mentality is a well-known aspect of British culture, highlighting the value placed on maintaining composure and not openly displaying emotions, especially in times of personal distress.

In this cultural context, individuals are encouraged to endure heartbreak with a sense of dignity and restraint. Public displays of intense emotion, particularly in matters of love and heartbreak, are often seen as undesirable. Instead, the emphasis is on internalizing one's feelings and dealing with them privately.

While this approach may appear stoic on the surface, it doesn't mean that the emotional experience of heartbreak is any less profound. It simply means that the cultural expression of that experience takes on a different form—one that values privacy and inner strength.

Now, let's talk about the emotions that come knocking with these experiences.

Physically, our bodies bear the weight of these feelings. When grappling with abandonment, we might experience sensations of tightness in our chest or knots in our stomach, signs that our body is responding to emotional distress. Loss can manifest in fatigue, appetite changes, and even physical pain. Heartbreak can lead to sleep disturbances, fatigue, and an overwhelming sense of heaviness (Davydov et al., 2011).

The impact on our emotional and physical well-being is profound. Abandonment, loss, and heartbreak can erode our self-esteem, dimming the light of our self-worth. They can blur our focus, hinder our decision-making, and cloud our perceptions.

But what happens within our brains when we grapple with these emotions? Neuroscience offers intriguing insights into the neurobiological basis of abandonment, loss, and heartbreak. Key regions of the brain, such as the amygdala, responsible for processing emotions like fear and sadness, and the prefrontal cortex, involved in emotional regulation, come into play.

Research reveals that when we confront these emotions, these brain regions light up with activity. The amygdala reacts to emotional stimuli, triggering the intense emotions we associate with abandonment and heartbreak. Meanwhile, the prefrontal cortex attempts to regulate these emotions, a battle that can leave us feeling emotionally drained (Jhonson, 2022).

Just as a broken bone regrows stronger, our emotional wounds possess growth potential. The path to healing involves acknowledging the pain, embracing our emotions, and nurturing our overall well-being. Building emotional resilience is not merely a choice; it is an absolute necessity to navigate the storms that life inevitably sends our way.

At its core, healing is about acknowledging the pain we've endured, facing our emotions with courage and compassion, and tending to the wounds that lie within. It's an active commitment to our well-being, a journey that fosters self-discovery and self-compassion.

Emotional resilience, on the other hand, is our ability to bounce back from adversity, to adapt to life's challenges with grace and determination. It's not just about surviving; it's about thriving despite the difficulties we encounter. When we actively work on building emotional resilience, we equip ourselves with the tools to face adversity head-on. We become akin to the sturdy oak tree that bends but does not break in the face of strong winds.

Just as a muscle grows stronger with exercise, our emotional muscles can develop through the challenges we face. Each emotional hurdle we overcome, each moment of healing, contributes to our growth as individuals. It's through these experiences that we discover our inner strength, resilience, and capacity for love and compassion.

In the chapters ahead, we'll dive into practical techniques, strategies, and insights that will guide you toward healing and resilience. We'll explore the stages of healing, the roots of abandonment issues, and strategies for addressing and healing these wounds. But for now, let this chapter serve as a stepping stone toward understanding the intricate labyrinth of abandonment, loss, and heartbreak.

As you embark on this exploration, consider this: Have you experienced moments of abandonment, loss, or heartbreak? How did they manifest in your life? Take these reflections with you as we journey through the chapters that lie ahead, ready to embrace healing and emotional resilience.

2

Navigating Abandonment Issues

"The scars of abandonment don't fade with time. That's a lie; they fade when we choose to heal."

— Unknown

Like hidden undercurrents, abandonment, and defection can shape the course of our lives and relationships.

Within these pages, we'll unravel the origins of abandonment issues, tracing their roots and understanding how they silently influence our experiences. We will explore the aftermath of past events marked by neglect, rejection, or loss events that continue to cast shadows on our self-worth and our capacity to trust and connect.

We'll uncover subtle signs of abandonment issues, recognizing their presence in our thoughts, emotions, and actions. By bringing these signs to light, we empower ourselves to mend these emotional wounds.

As we previously covered, abandonment stems from experiences of neglect, rejection, or loss during our formative years. These experiences, whether overt or subtle, lay the foundation for our relationship with ourselves and others.

Consider the story of famed poet Maya Angelou, who, as a child, experienced abandonment when her parents' marriage ended. She beautifully portrays it in her autobiographical book *I Know Why the Caged Bird Sings* (1999). The caged bird represents the trapped and silenced spirit, while the free bird soars with unbridled freedom. Angelou's narrative paints a vivid picture of a caged bird yearning for release from the confines of abandonment and trauma. This deep-seated guilt and sense of responsibility exemplify how abandonment issues can manifest in a child's psyche.

To understand the roots of abandonment issues, we must delve into the profound fears and insecurities that often accompany them. These issues can stem from the fear of being unloved, unwanted, or unworthy. They whisper in the recesses of our minds, shaping our self-perception and influencing our behavior in relationships.

Research in psychology tells us that these fears and insecurities often find their roots in our earliest attachments. Bowlby's groundbreaking work has shed light on how our infant-caregiver relationships profoundly shape our adult bonds.

Our childhood experiences serve as the lens through which we perceive and interact with the world as adults. These early encounters, be they positive or negative, become the templates for our adult relationships and influence our emotional responses.

Take the example of actress and humanitarian Audrey Hepburn. During the Nazi occupation, the Hepburn family, like countless others, experienced the devastating impact of war. Food shortages, rationing, and the constant threat of violence were daily realities. Hepburn's family, in particular, faced severe hardships. Her father was a member of the Dutch resistance, and Audrey herself became involved in acts of resistance, even delivering messages for the underground movement. These perilous activities placed her in constant danger.

Hepburn's childhood experiences under Nazi occupation had a profound and lasting impact on her adult perceptions of suffering and adversity. She witnessed the horrors of war, including the suffering of innocent children caught in its crossfire. These experiences left her with an enduring empathy for those in need, especially children who had been affected by conflict and poverty.

Hepburn's dedication to children in need manifested in her role as a UNICEF Goodwill Ambassador. She traveled extensively to regions ravaged by war, famine, and disease, bringing attention to the suffering of children and mobilizing resources for their aid. Her advocacy work helped raise awareness about the critical needs of vulnerable children in post-war Europe, Africa, Asia, and beyond.

Hepburn's experiences during World War II catalyzed her lifelong mission to alleviate the suffering of children. She believed that every child, regardless of their circumstances, deserved a chance at a better life. Her unwavering commitment to this cause exemplified the transformative power of personal experience, empathy, and a deep sense of compassion (Biography, 2021).

In her story, we find a testament to the resilience of the human spirit and the capacity for empathy and compassion to drive positive change in the world. Her legacy as both a cinematic icon and a humanitarian advocate continues to inspire generations to make a difference in the lives of children in need, echoing the enduring impact of her early experiences during wartime.

Nonetheless, it is necessary to understand that these results do not come alone. Hepburn's story is not a miracle; It is the result of a context of possibilities, personal work, and massive support.

So, what happens then when our ghosts from the past permeate our lives, and we do not have a solid context to battle them?

Consider the following scenario: A child experiences the abrupt separation of his parents, which leads to severe depression for the child. The mother and father engage in judicial conflicts, preventing the child from seeing their father frequently.

For kids, this announcement can feel like abandonment. They can't comprehend the complexities of adult relationships, and in their young mind, it seems as though their parents are leaving them behind.

As they grow older, these feelings of abandonment begin to manifest in their behavior. They become unusually clingy to friends, fearing that they will be left behind, much like their parents. Trust becomes a significant issue for them, and they find it hard to believe that anyone will stay in their life for the long term. These abandonment issues become a shadow that looms over their relationships and affects their ability to trust and connect with others.

In their romantic relationships, these people can potentially become overly possessive, smothering their partners with constant demands for reassurance. Their fear of abandonment often becomes a self-fulfilling prophecy, as their behavior drives partners away.

Most of us may not have had to go through the shocking and horrible experience of war like Audrey Hepburn did, but we have all fought some personal war. The vast majority of people have lost a loved one or a situation that we thought was ideal and, once it is dissolved, we have to grieve. All scars deserve to be healed, and all people deserve the opportunity to grow and become more emotionally evolved beings.

But the cure for these wounds is not discovered; it is built. May these pages be the scaffolding on which you assemble, dear reader, your healing.

May these stories serve as a common thread for the next pages, where we explore the consequences over time of abandonment, how to identify them, and how to create a diverse and healthy approach to closing once and for all the wounds of the past.

The Start Line

To start this journey, let's analyze how these issues can affect our relationships with others. They don't discriminate; they can parasitize all types of relationships, from romantic partnerships to friendships and even familial bonds.

In romantic relationships, these issues can be particularly pronounced. The fear of abandonment can manifest as jealousy, insecurity, and an overwhelming need for constant reassurance. These emotions often stem from early experiences of abandonment or rejection, leading people to question their partner's commitment and love. Research has shown that individuals with abandonment issues may struggle with trust, intimacy, and vulnerability in romantic partnerships, making it challenging to build and maintain a healthy connection (Fritscher, 2019).

Friendships can also be affected, as individuals with abandonment issues may struggle with feelings of inadequacy and fear of rejection in their social circles. They might find themselves overanalyzing interactions, constantly seeking validation, or withdrawing from friendships altogether to protect themselves from potential abandonment.

In familial relationships, abandonment issues can manifest as an intense need for validation and approval from parents or caregivers. Children who experienced abandonment or neglect during their formative years may carry these wounds into adulthood, seeking to fill the void left by early emotional scars. This can strain parent-child relationships and lead to codependent dynamics.

One of the core aspects of abandonment issues is the pervasive fear of rejection and defection. This fear can color our interactions with others, making it challenging to express our authentic selves and communicate our needs effectively. We may become overly accommodating, suppressing our own desires and boundaries to avoid potential rejection. Alternatively, we might adopt defensive behaviors, pushing people away before they have the chance to abandon us.

As you can see, these challenges arise from early past situations where we felt abandoned in some way. So, how exactly do these experiences shape and condition our present mindset?

Our past experiences serve as the crucible in which our emotional responses are forged. Consider this scenario: As a child, you experienced a significant abandonment, perhaps the divorce of your parents. This event imprints a profound emotional memory on your psyche. It shapes your understanding of relationships, trust, and vulnerability.

Fast-forward to your adult life, and you find yourself struggling with fear and insecurity in romantic relationships. You may not consciously connect your present emotions to that childhood experience, but the connection is there, lurking in the depths of your subconscious. Your past abandonment has left an indelible mark, influencing how you perceive and respond to the world around you.

One of the key mechanisms through which past experiences influence our present feelings in the context of abandonment issues is the phenomenon of triggering. Triggers are emotional landmines buried in our subconscious, waiting to be detonated by circumstances or interactions that echo our past wounds.

Imagine you're in a relationship, and your partner innocently mentions a change in their work schedule. Suddenly, you're flooded with anxiety and insecurity. What you might not realize is that this seemingly innocuous comment has triggered memories and emotions from your past experiences of abandonment. Your subconscious has drawn a parallel between this minor change and the fear of being left alone or unwanted.

Identifying These Issues

At this point, we've explored the deep-seated nature of abandonment issues, their origins, and their impact on our emotional landscape so far. Now, it's time to delve into the crucial task of recognizing these issues within ourselves and others. We will explore common behavioral and emotional signs:

- **Fear of rejection:** Abandonment issues frequently give rise to an overpowering fear of rejection. This fear can be so pervasive that it leads to a reluctance to form new relationships or an incessant need for reassurance within existing ones. People dealing with abandonment concerns usually interpret ambiguous social cues as indicators of rejection. This heightened sensitivity can exacerbate their fear and anxiety.

- **Difficulty trusting others:** Trust is the bedrock of healthy relationships. Yet, for those grappling with abandonment issues, trusting others can be an uphill battle. Past experiences of abandonment have left scars, making it challenging to extend trust fully. Research suggests that individuals with abandonment issues may exhibit hypervigilance for signs of potential betrayal (DiBartolo et al., 2004).

Think about a time when someone close to you let you down or betrayed your trust. If you find it challenging to trust others afterward, it's a sign that past experiences have influenced your ability to extend trust fully. This mistrust might make you guarded, leading to difficulties in forming deep connections.

- **Overly self-reliant**: Some individuals with abandonment issues respond by becoming overly self-reliant. They may hesitate to depend on others emotionally or avoid seeking assistance, believing that self-sufficiency is their shield against potential abandonment. Bowlby's (1989) research underscores the profound impact of early caregiving experiences on our ability to seek and accept support from others.

Consider a situation where you needed help or emotional support but hesitated to ask for it because you didn't want to burden others or feared rejection. This self-reliance might have caused you to shoulder your emotional burdens alone, believing that relying on yourself is the safest option.

- **Difficulty expressing emotions**: Reflect on moments when you've felt overwhelmed by emotions but found it challenging to express them. Maybe you kept your feelings bottled up to avoid appearing vulnerable or feared that sharing them would push others away.

Emotional expression can be a challenging terrain for those with abandonment issues. They may find it arduous to open up, share their feelings, or ask for help when needed. These challenges often stem from a fear of vulnerability, as emotional expression can feel like relinquishing control and potentially inviting rejection.

Addressing abandonment wounds requires a comprehensive strategy that encompasses the mind, body, and soul. It's about recognizing the wounds, understanding their origins, and nurturing your inner self back to a place of emotional well-being.

Inner-Child Healing

To begin, let's introduce the concept of *inner-child* healing. This therapeutic approach delves into the idea that the wounds we carry often stem from experiences in our early years. It's as if a part of us remains frozen in time, holding onto those painful moments. Inner child healing seeks to reconnect with that wounded inner self, offering understanding, love, and a chance to heal.

Now, you might be wondering, *Where do I start with inner-child healing?* While we'll touch on this subject here, if you wish to explore it more deeply, you can refer to my other book, *Healing Your Inner Child First*, which provides an extensive guide to this profoundly transformative process.

Central to the healing process is self-awareness. It's the ability to recognize when your abandonment wounds are influencing your thoughts, emotions, and behaviors. By shedding light on these patterns, you gain the power to change them. That's why we'll now discuss its significance in the context of healing these *inner children*. The following sections will also provide you with exercises and practices to help you become more attuned to your inner world. You'll learn to identify the triggers that set off emotional reactions related to abandonment, allowing you to respond with greater awareness and intention.

So, we are in a much clearer place than at the beginning: We now understand what these unpleasant emotions are, what their origin is, and how they affect our present emotions, behavior, and worldview.

Allow me to propose some simple and effective exercises to start working on awareness and understanding of these wounds.

One powerful method for healing abandonment issues involves the concept of self-compassion. It is about treating ourselves with the same kindness and understanding that we would offer to a dear friend. By acknowledging our pain, forgiving ourselves for any perceived shortcomings, and embracing our vulnerabilities, we can begin to heal. Self-awareness is equally vital, as it allows us to recognize when our abandonment wounds are influencing our thoughts, emotions, and behaviors. Yet, this is a skill we must develop with patience and commitment. Let me bring you some practical tips to practice and strengthen your self-compassion skills:

- **Meditation:** Consider exploring loving-kindness meditation, also known as *metta* meditation. Find a quiet space, close your eyes, and repeat phrases like, "May I be happy. May I be healthy. May I be safe. May I live with ease." Gradually, extend these wishes to others, including loved ones, acquaintances, and even those you may have conflicts with. This practice promotes self-compassion and compassion for others.

- **Positive affirmations:** Create a list of positive affirmations that resonate with you. These claims should focus on self-acceptance, self-worth, and self-love. For example, you might say, "I am deserving of love and happiness," or "I am enough just as I am." Repeat them daily to counteract negative self-talk.

To set you on the path of healing, here are some actionable steps you can take:

- **Mindfulness and grounding techniques:** Explore mindfulness practices and grounding techniques to help you stay present and manage anxiety or overwhelming emotions. Mindfulness meditation can improve emotional regulation and reduce the impact of abandonment triggers. Grounding exercises, such as the 5-4-3-2-1 technique (acknowledging five things you can see, four things you can touch, three things you can hear, two things you can smell, and one thing you can taste), can help you stay connected to the present moment.

- **Connect with supportive communities:** Seek out support groups or online communities where individuals share similar experiences with abandonment issues. Engaging with others who understand your struggles can be comforting and validating. These communities can also provide a platform for sharing coping strategies and insights.

- **Engage in joyful activities**: Do things that make you happy. This is an act of self-care, and it builds your sense of self. This allows you to develop a deeper sense of self-compassion and also to perceive your life as a happier experience. These things can be from diverse natures: arts, sports, walks in nature, social volunteering, or gardening. It has been broadly supported by clinical evidence that hobbies and preferred activities increase significantly the general well-being and happiness of people who practice them over those who don't (Pressman et al., 2009).

When you turn to the next page of this book, take it as an act that symbolizes the beginning of a new stage in your life, one of healing, peace, and forgiveness.

Your Free Bonus: Unlock Self-Compassion Right Now!

I am deeply committed to offering you more than just words on a page. That's why, throughout this book, I've included a series of thoughtfully designed free bonuses to support you on your journey of abandonment recovery. These are your moments of pause—created to help you nurture and care for yourself as you work through each chapter. You can download them whenever you're ready— right away, or at the perfect moment for you.

The first of these gifts is The Self-Compassion Workbook. Above, we've already touched briefly on self-compassion, and later in this book, it will come up more often, but I wanted to give you a little kickstart. This resource is here to help you cultivate kindness and understanding toward yourself as you navigate the healing process.

Get access to your workbook now by visiting: https://booksforbetterlife.com/abandonment-recovery or scan the QR code:

3

The Five Stages of Abandonment Healing

"When we go deeper into every experience and emotion; especially the painful ones, we tap into the source of our greatest hidden gifts."

— Ulonda Faye

Just as a diamond is formed under pressure, our deepest hidden gifts often emerge when we confront and heal from the wounds of abandonment.

In this chapter, we will delve into the five stages of abandonment healing, drawing inspiration from renowned psychologist Elisabeth Kübler-Ross's model of grief from her book *On Grief and Grieving: Finding the Meaning of Grief through the Five Stages of Loss* (2005). The stages are denial, anger, bargaining, depression, and acceptance. These stages are not a linear path, but rather a journey through the emotional landscape of healing, and they hold the power to transform our lives.

Before we begin our exploration of these stages, let me share an anecdote from my work as a clinical psychologist. I once worked with a patient who had experienced profound abandonment in childhood. Their journey through these stages was a testament to the resilience of the human spirit.

In the denial stage, they initially struggled to acknowledge the impact of their past experiences on their current struggles. However, as we gently explored their history and the emotional walls they had built, they began to embrace the reality of their pain.

Anger emerged as a powerful force in their healing process. They expressed outrage at the circumstances that had led to their abandonment, and we worked together to channel this anger constructively, using it as a catalyst for change.

Bargaining followed as they sought to understand their past and make sense of the pain. They engaged in inner dialogues, asking questions like, "Why did this happen to me?" This stage was marked by introspection and a deep quest for meaning.

Depression was perhaps the most challenging phase for my patient. The weight of their past experiences bore down on them, and they grappled with sadness, isolation, and a sense of hopelessness. Yet, within this darkness, seeds of healing were planted.

Finally, acceptance dawned. My patient began to embrace

their past, not as a source of shame but as a wellspring of strength and resilience. Their journey through the five stages had transformed them, and they emerged with a newfound sense of self-worth and purpose.

In this chapter, we will walk alongside individuals like my patient, exploring each stage's emotional landscape and the unique challenges they present. We will draw from psychological research and practical strategies to navigate these stages effectively.

The Five Stages

Denial

The first stage, denial, often serves as a protective shield against the overwhelming pain of abandonment. At this point, individuals may find themselves in a state of disbelief, unable or unwilling to acknowledge the depth of their emotional wounds. Denial can manifest as a defense mechanism, allowing individuals to temporarily avoid the intense emotions that accompany abandonment issues.

At this stage, we might find ourselves grappling with a range of emotions, from shock and disbelief to numbness. It's as if a protective shield has been erected around our hearts, guarding us from the rawness of our pain.

In my journey through abandonment healing, I vividly remember the denial stage. I clung desperately to the hope that the relationship I cherished hadn't truly ended. Even though the signs were evident, I couldn't bear to confront the abyss of my emotions. Denial, as it does for many, shielded me momentarily from the impending tidal wave of grief.

It's crucial to recognize that denial is a natural response to emotional trauma. During this stage, individuals may question the validity of their feelings or minimize the impact of past experiences. This denial acts as a shield against the overwhelming pain, allowing us to temporarily avoid confronting our abandonment wounds.

Anger

As denial gradually gives way, a surge of anger often emerges. Individuals may feel anger at themselves for their perceived inadequacies or at those they believe abandoned or hurt them. It's important to understand that anger is a powerful and necessary part of the healing process.

Anger serves several purposes during this stage. It can act as a catalyst for change, motivating individuals to address their abandonment wounds actively. It also provides an outlet for the pain and frustration that have long been suppressed. Therapy and support groups can be invaluable during this phase, helping individuals channel their anger constructively and navigate this tumultuous stage.

We might direct this anger outward, aiming it at those we perceive as responsible for our pain. It's a fierce, fiery emotion that can feel overwhelming. Alternatively, we may turn this anger inward, chastising ourselves for perceived shortcomings.

During my abandonment healing journey, anger emerged with astonishing intensity. I found myself enraged at my ex-partner for causing me such heartache. But as I delved deeper, I realized that beneath that anger lay a profound sadness—the recognition of the loss I had endured.

Bargaining

In the bargaining stage, individuals often seek to make sense of their past experiences and the pain they've endured. This stage is marked by inner dialogues and questions such as, *Why did this happen to me?* or, *If only I had done things differently*. Bargaining is an attempt to regain a sense of control and find meaning amid suffering.

This, just like the others, is a natural response to the confusion and pain of abandonment. It signifies a willingness to engage with one's emotions and past experiences on a deeper level. While it may not provide definitive answers, this stage invites introspection and self-exploration, laying the groundwork for further healing.

The bargaining stage invites us to seek meaning and make sense of our experiences. We engage in inner dialogues, attempting to negotiate our way out of pain. We may make promises to ourselves or even to a higher power, believing that by doing so, we can rewrite the narrative of our lives.

I recall a moment when I bargained with myself, promising to change, to become a better version of myself, in hopes of winning back a love I believed I couldn't live without. This stage revealed the depths of my attachment and the fear of losing a part of my identity tied to that relationship.

Depression

Depression, the fourth stage, can be one of the most challenging phases of abandonment healing. It is marked by a deep sense of sadness, isolation, and often a feeling of hopelessness. Individuals may grapple with the weight of their past experiences and the realization of the profound impact these experiences have had on their lives.

During this stage, it's essential to emphasize that depression is not a sign of weakness but a testament to the depth of one's emotional journey. Therapy and support are particularly crucial during this phase, providing individuals with a safe space to express their emotions and seek guidance.

During this stage, we confront the weight of our past experiences, and the reality of the impact these experiences have had on our lives can be overwhelming.

In my own journey, depression became an unwelcome companion. The weight of my emotions, the sense of abandonment, and the bleakness of the future often left me feeling as though I were sinking into an abyss. Yet, it was in this darkness that I discovered the seeds of transformation.

Acceptance

Finally, we reach the final stage, acceptance. It represents a profound transformation. It is the culmination of the healing journey, where individuals begin to embrace their past experiences not as sources of shame but as wellsprings of strength and resilience. Acceptance signifies a newfound sense of self-worth and purpose.

We cease to deny the pain or attempt to bargain for a different outcome. Instead, we integrate the experience into our identity.

Yet, it does not mean forgetting or erasing the past. Instead, it involves integrating these experiences into one's identity and using them as a source of empowerment. Acceptance allows people to move forward with a sense of self-compassion and a commitment to building emotional resilience.

In my journey, acceptance was a revelation—a recognition that the end of that relationship was not the end of me. It was a beginning, a chance to rediscover my true self and embrace a future filled with possibilities.

The Transition Process

Transitioning through the stages of abandonment healing can be a challenging journey. However, there are practical strategies rooted in scientific research that can make this process more manageable.

In the first phase, it's important to recognize that denial is a natural response to emotional trauma. This stage acts as a shield, protecting us from overwhelming emotions that may be too painful to confront. Acknowledging your feelings is the first step, and one effective way to do this is through journaling. Research suggests that expressive writing can significantly reduce the impact of emotional trauma (Niles et al., 2013). When you put your thoughts and emotions on paper, it helps you make sense of your experiences and gradually move toward acceptance.

As you transition to the next stage, you may find that channeling your anger through physical activities is highly beneficial. Scientific studies have demonstrated that exercise is a powerful tool for outrage management (Dettori et al., 2019):

- One option is cardiovascular exercises, like running, brisk walking, or cycling. These activities can be excellent outlets for anger, as they get your heart rate up and trigger the release of endorphins, which are natural mood lifters. They also offer a meditative aspect, allowing you to clear your mind and focus on the rhythm of your movements.

- Strength training, including weightlifting and resistance exercises, is another effective way to manage anger. These exercises can help you channel your frustration into lifting weights or pushing against resistance. The physical exertion can be cathartic and empowering, leaving you feeling stronger both mentally and physically.

- Yoga and tai chi are mind-body practices that combine physical postures with breath control and meditation.

These disciplines encourage self-awareness, mindfulness, and relaxation. They can be particularly helpful in reducing anger by promoting emotional balance and self-control.

- Martial arts, like karate or kickboxing, offer an opportunity to express anger in a controlled and disciplined environment. These practices teach self-defense techniques while emphasizing respect and self-discipline. Engaging in martial arts can provide a healthy outlet for anger while also boosting self-confidence.

Ultimately, the choice of exercise should align with your personal preferences and physical abilities. The key is to find an activity that allows you to release anger and enjoy its broader benefits!

Additionally, therapy or support groups can provide a safe and constructive space to explore and address your anger. The benefits of group therapy for anger management have been highlighted in numerous research. In these settings, you can learn valuable techniques for managing your anger and gain insights from others who may be experiencing similar emotions (Sukhodolsky et al., 2019).

The bargaining stage is a time for self-reflection and exploring healthier paths to fulfill your desires. This phase is deeply intertwined with psychology, as it involves understanding the motivations behind your bargaining behavior. Self-awareness is a crucial component of this process. Mindfulness meditation can assist you in staying present and preventing excessive rumination. Through this meditation approach, you can gain clarity on your desires and discern more adaptive ways to achieve them.

Moving into the depression stage can be incredibly challenging, but it's essential to practice self-compassion during this time. Research suggests that self-compassion is highly effective in navigating depression. Instead of criticizing yourself for feeling depressed, approach this stage with kindness and understanding (Körner et al., 2015).

Finally, in the acceptance stage, the focus shifts toward self-discovery and growth. This stage is not an endpoint but a foundation for emotional resilience and a future filled with hope. Engaging in mindfulness meditation, yoga, or creative pursuits can help you reconnect with your true self. These practices have been shown to improve emotional well-being in numerous scientific studies. They provide a space for self-expression, self-awareness, and personal growth.

Healing Journey

As we have learned throughout these pages, healing from abandonment is not a linear path; it's a series of stages, each with its unique challenges and opportunities for growth. To help you navigate these stages, allow me to provide you with practical techniques and coping strategies tailored to each phase of your journey.

Throughout your healing journey, two steadfast companions will be self-compassion and self-care. These elements are powerful practices that will support you in every stage of recovery.

Self-compassion is your gentle guide, teaching you to treat yourself with kindness, understanding, and patience. It's about acknowledging your pain without judgment, forgiving yourself for any perceived shortcomings, and embracing your vulnerabilities. Self-care, on the other hand, is the art of nourishing your physical, emotional, and mental well-being. It's about recognizing that you are deserving of care and taking intentional steps to meet your needs. These notions are deeply interconnected, so we can develop them simultaneously.

The following strategies are designed to provide you with tools to navigate the complexities of each stage with a sense of self-compassion and self-care, empowering you to move forward:

- **Dedicate time for yourself:** Establish self-care routines that prioritize your well-being. This might include daily walks, meditation, or simply taking time for a warm bath.

- **Manage anger healthily:** Engage in physical activities like jogging, dancing, or hitting a punching bag to release pent-up anger in a nutritive way.

- **Learn effective communication:** These techniques are paramount to expressing your feelings without escalating conflicts. "I" statements can be particularly helpful. This form of communication focuses on expressing your feelings, thoughts, and needs, rather than making accusations or blaming others, and they are highly useful in conflict resolution and effective communication. Here's an example: Instead of saying, "You never listen to me, and it's frustrating," which can come across as accusatory, you can use an "I" statement like this: "I feel frustrated when I perceive that my thoughts aren't considered." This way, you are smartly shifting the focus from blaming the other person to expressing your feelings and needs, making it a more constructive way to communicate since the other person will be more likely to listen to you, take a proactive posture, and negotiate.

As you explore new possibilities and set goals for yourself, celebrate each step of progress along the way. This positive reinforcement is essential for building emotional resilience and maintaining a sense of hope for the future. Embracing the strategies rooted in psychology and supported by scientific evidence equips you with valuable tools on your healing journey.

By employing these strategies, you not only heal from abandonment but also emerge stronger, wiser, and more resilient than ever before. Remember that your healing journey is unique, and it's okay to seek professional support when needed. With time, patience, and self-compassion, you can navigate these stages and emerge on the other side with a deeper understanding of yourself and your inner strength.

The next chapter will take you deeper into two of the pivotal stages of abandonment healing. You'll explore the protective nature of these and how they are an integral part of your healing process.

Bonus: Your Mood Tracker for Emotional Breakthroughs

Before diving into the transformative 5 Stages of Abandonment, I'm excited to share a valuable tool to support you: Your Mood Tracker.

Tracking your mood isn't just about recording feelings; it's about embracing your progress and identifying patterns that lead to breakthroughs. By logging your emotions, you'll create a personal record of resilience that highlights the growth you might not immediately notice. This practice empowers you to stay connected with yourself and celebrate small victories, which are crucial in your recovery journey.

This Mood Tracker is more than a log—it's a mirror of your courage and a reminder of how far you've come. Start today, and let it guide you as you reclaim your emotional well-being and resilience.

Ready to chart your growth? Get immediate access by visiting: https://booksforbetterlife.com/abandonment-recovery or scan the QR code:

4

Embracing Denial and Acceptance

"The greatest glory in living lies not in never falling, but in rising every time we fall."

— Nelson Mandela

In the tapestry of human emotions, few threads are as paradoxical and intertwined as denial and acceptance. These two stages of abandonment healing often appear as opposites, yet they are inextricably linked, each playing a unique role in the intricate journey toward emotional resilience.

In the depths of our exploration into the profound stages of denial and acceptance, let me introduce you to a remarkable character: one of my patients who lived a life marked by indomitable courage and resilience. His story, like so many others, embodies the very essence of the human spirit's ability to overcome the darkest of tribulations.

A Story

This person's journey began in the crucible of war, where the rubble-strewn streets were his playground. A refugee from a land torn asunder by conflict, he embarked on a treacherous odyssey that led him to a new country. Yet, he and his family arrived here with nothing but the heavy baggage of his past.

For him, denial became a constant companion, a fortress constructed around his psyche to ward off the relentless memories of his tumultuous childhood. In a new land, he sought to create a life untethered from the shadows of his history. He convinced himself that the horrors he endured were mere phantoms, exercised by the passage of time.

However, the emotional toll of his experiences lingered like an unrelenting undertow beneath calm waters. Anxiety, though buried deep, whispered its presence in the hushed moments of solitude. Denial was his shield, but it also perpetuated the cycle of unease, like a fire smoldering beneath the surface.

It wasn't until he found his way to my clinic, after a year of unwavering therapy and soul-searching, that the transformation began. His journey serves as a testament to the complex interplay of emotions that define the stages of healing from abandonment, loss, and heartbreak.

In his story, denial was not a mere refusal to confront reality; it was a coping mechanism, a lifeline that allowed him to survive and navigate the daunting seas of a new beginning. It was a sanctuary where he could tend to the wounds of his past at his own pace.

But it was also a stage, a necessary cocoon in which he cocooned his emotions, protecting them until he was ready to face the harsh light of acceptance. And when that moment arrived, after a year of tireless self-exploration, therapy, and reflection, the transformation was nothing short of miraculous.

His journey, like the one we are about to embark upon in this chapter, showcases the intricate dance between denial and acceptance. It underscores the profound significance of these stages in the healing process. Denial was his starting point, his way of coping with the unbearable weight of his past. And acceptance, when it finally arrived, became the foundation upon which his emotional resilience was built.

In the pages that follow, we will embark on a profound exploration of these seemingly contradictory yet harmonious stages: denial and acceptance. We will traverse the complex landscapes of the human psyche, guided by real-life stories, scientific insights, and therapeutic wisdom.

We'll first delve into the protective nature of denial, demystifying its role in the healing process. By examining its nuances, we'll understand why denial often serves as a necessary cocoon before the soul can unfurl its wings of acceptance.

From there, our journey will lead us to the transformative shores of acceptance. We'll discover the incredible power of embracing one's truth and making peace with the past.

As we navigate the stories and insights within these pages, remember that your own journey may mirror the patients I shared earlier or may take an entirely different path. However, the lessons within are universal, offering a guiding light for those traversing the challenging terrain of abandonment healing.

Denial, Denial, Denial

Denial, in psychological terms, is a defense mechanism that human beings employ to shield themselves from emotions and realities that they perceive as too distressing to confront head-on. It's like a psychological bouncer that stands guard at the entrance to our consciousness, filtering out emotions that might threaten to overwhelm us.

In the context of abandonment, loss, or heartbreak, denial manifests as a refusal to accept the full weight of the experience. It's a way of saying to yourself, *I cannot process all of this right now*. This mechanism temporarily veils the harsh truths of our situation, giving us some respite from the emotional onslaught.

Denial provides a vital psychological buffer. It allows individuals to pace themselves in processing the often traumatic events they've endured. Like a thermostat regulating extreme temperatures, denial dials down the emotional intensity to a level that feels more manageable.

Operant conditioning, a cornerstone of behavioral psychology introduced by B. F. Skinner in the mid-20th century, plays a fundamental role in shaping human behavior. This concept revolves around the idea that behavior can be altered through its outcomes. To illustrate, consider a real-world scenario in a workplace: An employee consistently meets project deadlines and delivers high-quality work. In response, the employer provides positive reinforcement in the form of a monthly recognition award and a bonus, effectively encouraging the employee to maintain this exemplary performance.

Conversely, operant conditioning can also be used to curtail undesired behaviors. In a parental context, imagine a child who frequently throws tantrums to get a desired toy. The parents decide to apply negative reinforcement by withholding access to the toy until the child behaves appropriately. In this way, the child learns that throwing tantrums will not yield the desired result and gradually ceases this disruptive behavior.

These examples demonstrate how operant conditioning, with its principles of rewards and punishments, is applicable to diverse settings and can be a powerful tool for modifying behavior effectively.

Denial can manifest in various aspects of life, extending beyond personal relationships. For example, someone who receives a grim medical diagnosis might initially reject the information, seeking second or third opinions in hopes of a different outcome. Or, in the face of a job loss, a person might continue their daily routine, as if nothing has changed, believing that they'll soon find another opportunity.

These examples underscore how denial can infiltrate different spheres of our existence. It's not a conscious decision but rather an instinctual response to overwhelming emotions.

There is no fixed timeline, as everyone's capacity to cope with distressing emotions differs. Still, recognizing when denial has persisted too long, and it's time to move forward to the next stage is crucial for healthy emotional processing. Here are some signs that can indicate when denial may have become an obstacle to healing:

- If someone constantly avoids thinking about or discussing the event or situation, it may be a sign that they are stuck in denial. Healthy denial allows for temporary avoidance, but when it becomes a long-term pattern, it can hinder healing.

- During this stage, individuals may suppress their emotions or put on a façade of being unaffected. If there's a consistent inability to express or acknowledge emotions related to the experience, it may indicate prolonged denial.

- It can keep people locked in a state of inertia, where they resist making necessary changes or adjustments in their lives. If someone is unable to take steps to adapt to their new reality, it may be time to move forward.

- Escapist behaviors such as excessive substance use, overeating, or compulsive behaviors can be signs of denial. These behaviors are attempts to numb or distract from painful emotions.

- If someone withdraws from social interactions and isolates themselves for an extended period, it may indicate that they are stuck in denial. We are social beings, and we do need support from others.

- Unresolved emotions and persistent denial can contribute to mental health issues such as anxiety, depression, or post-traumatic stress disorder.

Transitioning from denial to acceptance is a nuanced and often challenging process. While this journey is deeply personal and varies from individual to individual, several practical techniques can gently guide readers toward the eventual acceptance stage.

From Denial to Acceptance

As I previously mentioned, encouraging mindful self-reflection is an essential step in the transition toward acceptance.

You can begin by setting aside moments of quiet reflection each day. During these periods, you should focus on your emotional experiences without trying to change or analyze them. The goal is to simply acknowledge your feelings as they arise. Over time, this practice can help people become more attuned to their emotional landscape and pave the way for a healthier transition.

Journaling is also a powerful tool for self-expression and the exploration of hidden feelings. Readers can engage in journaling exercises to facilitate the transition from denial to acceptance. Here are some suggested prompts to get started:

- Write about a recent event or memory that triggered strong emotions. Describe these emotions in detail.

- Reflect on the ways in which denial has manifested in your life. Have you noticed patterns of avoidance or suppression?

- Imagine a conversation with your inner self. What would you say to yourself about the emotions you've been denying?

- Explore moments of resilience and strength in your life. How did you overcome challenges in the past?

I once worked with a courageous teenager who had suffered severe bullying at high school. The emotional scars ran deep, and for a long time, she was ensnared in the web of denial, unable to confront the pain she had endured. She blamed herself for the bullying, believing she was somehow responsible for the torment she endured.

However, as we embarked on the journey toward acceptance, self-compassion emerged as a beacon of hope for her. Together, we explored the importance of self-kindness. She began to acknowledge that she was not to blame for the actions of others. Through our sessions, she learned to embrace her imperfections and recognize that she was deserving of love and understanding, just like anyone else.

Self-Compassion Goes a Long Way

Incorporating these strategies can gradually shift the emotional landscape from one of self-blame and denial to one of self-acceptance and healing. Self-compassion is the bridge that helps individuals traverse the challenging terrain of denial and arrive at the shores of acceptance, where true healing can begin.

Let me delve a little deeper into this self-compassion thing.

Far from putting ourselves in the victim's place, the sense of self-compassion helps us embrace ourselves in moments where anger, frustration, or pain can cause us to lash out at ourselves; it stimulates patience and understanding of one's pain and is important for managing the stages of grief effectively and humanely. Below, I share some exercises that will help you cultivate compassion.

Exercise 1: The Self-Kindness Journal

- **Objective:** Encourage yourself to practice self-kindness, and acknowledge your suffering with tenderness.

- **Instructions:** Each day, set aside a few minutes to write in your journal. Reflect on a challenging or painful experience you had that day. Write down how it made you feel and any self-critical thoughts that arose. Then, consciously replace those self-critical thoughts with compassionate and understanding statements. For example, if you were too hard on yourself for making a mistake, replace it with, "It's okay to make mistakes; they are growth opportunities."

Exercise 2: Acknowledging Imperfections

- **Objective:** Help yourself embrace your imperfections and understand that they are a natural part of being human.

- **Instructions:** Make a list of your perceived imperfections or things you've been critical of about yourself. Then, next to each imperfection, write down a positive aspect or strength that balances it out. For example, if you feel you're too introverted, write down how being introverted allows you to be a good listener.

Exercise 3: Self-Compassion Mantras

- **Objective:** Provide yourself with powerful self-compassion mantras to use during challenging moments.

- **Instructions:** Create a list of self-compassion mantras or affirmations that resonate with you. These could include phrases like, "I am worthy of love and understanding," or "I deserve kindness, even in difficult times." Keep this list handy, and when you catch yourself being self-critical, repeat one of these mantras to yourself. You can turn to them, especially in challenging or difficult times, as a ground wire.

As we conclude this chapter on embracing denial and acceptance, I want to leave you with actionable steps to actively engage with the content and start applying these principles to your life.

1. Begin by acknowledging that it's okay to be where you are in your healing journey. Treat yourself with kindness and understanding, just as you would a dear friend facing a similar struggle. Remember that self-compassion is a powerful tool for shifting from denial to acceptance.

2. Consider keeping a journal to document your thoughts and feelings as you navigate these stages. Journaling can be a therapeutic way to process your emotions, identify patterns, and track your progress over time.

3. If you find that denial has become a prolonged defense mechanism, or if you're struggling to transition toward acceptance, don't hesitate to seek professional guidance. Therapy can provide a safe and supportive space to explore your emotions and facilitate a healthy transition.

Key takeaways to keep in mind:

- Denial serves as a protective shield that allows individuals to process trauma at a manageable pace. It shields us from overwhelming emotions and can be a vital phase in the healing journey.

- Recognizing the presence of denial is the first step toward embracing the acceptance stage. Prolonged denial can hinder progress, making it essential to understand when it's time to move forward.

- Mindful self-reflection, journaling, and seeking professional support are practical techniques for gently transitioning from denial to acceptance.

- Self-compassion plays a pivotal role in navigating these stages. It involves treating ourselves with kindness, acknowledging imperfections, and reframing negative self-talk.

I invite you to continue your healing journey by moving on to the next chapter, where we will explore the complex emotions of anger and bargaining, understanding how they can be harnessed for growth and resilience. Together, we will uncover practical strategies to navigate these stages and move closer to the ultimate goal of acceptance and healing.

5

Transforming Anger and Bargaining

"I saw clearly that so long as I was still a human being and not nothingness, I was alive and so could suffer, be angry, and feel shame at my actions."

— Fyodor Dostoevsky

Anger is definitely one of the more challenging emotions and plays a profound role in the human experience. It is a psychological response, a signal from within, alerting us to boundaries crossed, values challenged, and needs unmet. It serves as a regulator, a sentinel that calls attention to the injustices and frustrations we encounter in our lives.

Yet, as with any powerful force, anger has its nuances and its limits. It can grow unchecked, evolving into a trigger for violence and aggression. In this chapter, we explore its origins, purposes, the threshold at which this intense emotion becomes destructive, and how to recognize this perilous territory.

Within these pages, we embark on a journey through the stages of anger and bargaining. We'll delve deep into the psychological landscape, exploring the mechanisms that underlie these emotions. We'll uncover the roots of anger, the triggers that set it ablaze, and the constructive avenues for its expression.

Throughout this chapter, I invite you to embrace the potential for growth and healing that resides within the stages of anger and bargaining. It is a journey through the crucible of human emotion, a path illuminated by the wisdom of those who have trodden it before us.

So, as we step forward into this matter, let us remember that, in the realm of the human psyche, every emotion, even anger, holds the potential for profound change and healing. It is a testament to our resilience, our capacity for growth, and our innate human spirit.

The Roots of Anger

Within the depths of human emotion, anger, and bargaining emerge as poignant responses to one of life's most challenging trials: abandonment, loss, or heartbreak. These emotions, often viewed as turbulent waters to navigate, possess an intricate evolutionary lineage deeply rooted in our survival mechanisms.

Consider the essence of these emotions as an evolutionary blueprint etched into our very DNA. For our ancestors, the bonds forged within tribes and communities were integral to survival. Being abandoned, losing a loved one, or experiencing heartbreak were not merely personal tragedies; they were potential threats to the tribe's cohesion and, consequently, their collective and even personal survival.

In this context, anger emerged as a guardian, a response that alerted individuals to the perceived injustice of abandonment or loss. It served as a call to action—a signal that boundaries had been crossed, values had been violated, and an effort was required to restore the delicate balance within the tribe.

Within the crucible of abandonment or loss, feelings of powerlessness and frustration often surge to the forefront. These emotions, accompanied by the relentless desire to regain control, ignite the stage of bargaining. In essence, bargaining is an attempt to negotiate with the context, a plea to reverse the course of events, and a quest to reconquer what has been lost.

It is a primal response—an instinctive reach toward a return to the familiar, the comfortable, and the secure. It is, at its core, a testament to the enduring human spirit, a declaration that we will not be defeated by adversity.

Yet, as with many aspects of the human experience, the line between a healthy response and a harmful one is both fine and elusive. Healthy responses to anger and bargaining can manifest as assertive efforts to communicate, seek resolution, or adapt to new circumstances. These are actions that foster growth and healing, propelling us forward through the tumultuous terrain of emotions.

However, the same fervor that drives these responses can, when unchecked, transform into a relentless pursuit of the unattainable—a quest to reconquer a person or thing that has moved beyond our reach. This can become a self-destructive cycle, leading to prolonged suffering and stagnation.

A Story

In the quiet of my counseling room, I've had the privilege of bearing witness to the stories of individuals who have journeyed through the labyrinthine emotions of anger and bargaining.

There, a mother found solace in sharing the most harrowing chapter of her life. She had suffered the unthinkable: the traumatic loss of her child in a devastating car accident. As she recounted the heart-wrenching details, it was clear that grief had enveloped her entire existence.

Yet, amidst the depths of her grief, anger emerged as a tough companion. The person responsible for the accident had not only shattered her world but had also ignited a searing rage within her. The desire for vengeance, the need to inflict harm on the one who had taken her child, became a consuming fire.

In this crucible of anger born from grief, my patient grappled with the overwhelming intensity of her emotions. The anger, while a natural response to injustice, was a relentless storm that threatened to consume her. It was a testament to the profound complexity of human emotion, where anger, fueled by loss, could become a challenging adversary in the midst of traumatic grief.

TRANSFORMING ANGER AND BARGAINING

Anger and the desire to harm those who have inflicted pain on us is a natural response to grief, and we must understand it for what it is: a stage of the experience. However, it is important to highlight that these sensations and desires driven by anger can be powerful, like the ones my patient felt. In this case, it is necessary to seek help in our environment to be able to manage this anger in a healthy way, since although it is natural to experience anger, we cannot use her as an excuse to hurt others. Yet, these are some tips that can help you manage these emotions:

- Keep a personal journal where you can freely express your anger and desires without judgment. Writing down your thoughts and feelings can provide an outlet for processing these intense emotions.

- Try deep breathing exercises and relaxation techniques to calm your anger. Slow, deep breaths can help reduce anger's intensity and give you a sense of emotional control.

- Engage in physical activities like jogging, walking, or yoga to release built-up tension and anger. Exercise promotes the release of endorphins, which can boost your mood.

- Create and repeat positive affirmations that promote self-compassion and self-forgiveness. For example, say to yourself, *I am working through my anger in healthy ways*, or, *I choose to let go of thoughts of harm*.

- Try visualization exercises where you imagine letting go of anger and replacing it with feelings of peace and forgiveness. Visualization can be a powerful tool for changing your emotional state.

- Consider creative forms of expression like art, music, or writing to channel your anger constructively. Creative activities can help you process your emotions without causing harm.

Another Story

In a starkly different setting, another patient faced a crisis of an entirely different nature. The financial ruin of their once-thriving company had brought them to the precipice of despair. This person, a passionate entrepreneur, was confronted not only with the loss of their business but also with an overwhelming anger directed inward.

They blamed themselves and their business partners for the decisions that had led to this precipitous downfall. Anger coursed through their veins like wildfire, a relentless force that seemed to consume all rational thought. Every misstep and perceived failure fueled the flames of self-directed fury.

As the embers of rage smoldered, this patient found the strength and determination to rebuild. It was not an easy process, nor was it immediate, but over time, they harnessed their anger as a driving force for transformation.

First, this person engaged in deep self-reflection. They began by dissecting the decisions and actions that had led to the financial downfall. This introspection was not an exercise in self-blame but an objective assessment of what went wrong. They sought to understand the root causes of their business's collapse, recognizing that anger alone wouldn't provide solutions.

Next, they turned to education and self-improvement. This patient eagerly sought knowledge and expertise in areas where they had previously lacked. They attended seminars, read books, and consulted with mentors who could provide guidance. This pursuit of wisdom was fueled by their determination to never repeat the same mistakes.

They also prioritized resilience-building practices. Meditation and mindfulness played a significant role in quelling the destructive force of anger.

Perhaps most importantly, this patient shifted their perspective on failure. They realized that failure was not a final destination but a stepping stone on the path to success. Every misstep, every financial setback, became an invaluable lesson. This mindset shift allowed them to move forward with a sense of purpose and resilience.

These stories serve as reminders that anger, while often viewed as tumultuous and negative, can be a force for both destruction and transformation. In the face of grief and financial ruin, it takes on different forms, challenging us to navigate its complexities and harness its energy for healing and renewal.

"I" Statements

As we delve further into the chapter, we explore the various ways in which anger and bargaining intersect with our emotional landscapes. These patient stories are not just narratives; they are windows into the human experience, mirrors reflecting the strength and resilience that reside within us all.

Anger serves as a signal that something is amiss, a boundary has been crossed, or a value has been compromised. By learning to express anger assertively, individuals can convey their needs and feelings while maintaining respect for themselves and others.

One powerful technique is "I" statements—already addressed in the previous chapter.

Rephrasing a sentence so that it means the same thing but reaches the interlocutor effectively can be a tricky task, so let's see how we can learn to make these "I" statements to achieve more effective communication. Let's see an example of this particular emotion below:

Begin by thinking of a recent situation or interaction where you felt upset, hurt, or frustrated. It could be a conflict with a friend, family member, coworker, or partner. Write down a brief description of this situation. Then, pinpoint the emotions you experienced during the situation. Were you feeling angry, sad, disappointed, anxious, or something else? List the emotions you felt.

Consider what needs of yours weren't met in this situation. Needs can include things like respect, understanding, validation, or support. Identify the specific needs that were unfulfilled. Now, it's time to create your "I" statement.

Follow this format: *I feel* [emotion] *when* [describe the situation] *because I need* [state your unmet need].

For example:

- *I feel frustrated when my coworker interrupts me during meetings because I need the opportunity to express my ideas.*

- *I feel hurt when my partner cancels our plans at the last minute because I need reliability and trust in our relationship.*

Channeling Your Anger

Healthy outlets for anger can serve as release valves, preventing the buildup of unresolved emotions. Physical activities, journaling, or even engaging in creative pursuits can provide avenues for channeling anger into productive expressions.

Negotiation isn't limited to external dealings; it also involves negotiating with oneself. When grappling with anger and bargaining, the ability to find healthier ways to cope becomes paramount. This self-negotiation is an introspective process that requires self-awareness and resilience.

One effective strategy is mindfulness, which enables individuals to observe their thoughts and emotions without judgment. By acknowledging anger and bargaining without attaching labels like "good" or "bad," one can gain a deeper understanding of these emotions and how they manifest.

Additionally, reframing negative thoughts and beliefs can be a transformative negotiation tool. Instead of viewing setbacks as insurmountable obstacles, we can learn to see them as opportunities for growth and learning. This shift in perspective will significantly impact how anger and bargaining are processed.

To illustrate, allow me to propose an example of how to reframe negative thoughts and beliefs below.

Imagine you have an intrusive thought like this one: *I can't handle the challenges in my life right now. It's too much.* As soon as you identify it, try to replace it with something that reflects self-compassion and love like, *While these challenges are tough, they are also opportunities for me to learn and grow. I've faced difficult situations before, and each time, I've become stronger and more resilient. I can handle this.*

Why Set Boundaries?

Boundaries are the lines we draw to define our limits, the invisible fences that separate our needs, emotions, and values from those of others. During the phases of anger and bargaining, these edges become essential to maintaining our sense of self.

Creating them is an act of self-compassion, a commitment to preserving your emotional equilibrium. It involves a delicate dance of self-awareness, assertiveness, and empathy. Healthy boundaries serve as a buffer against overwhelming emotions, preventing you from being consumed by anger or bargaining.

Consider the story of the mother who lost her child. In the depths of her grief and anger, she recognized the need to set boundaries with those around her. She communicated her emotional limits and asked for the support she required without compromising her well-being.

Similarly, the individual facing financial ruin implemented boundaries within their business partnerships. They communicated their needs and established clear expectations, ensuring that their emotions were respected and their decisions were made with a sense of agency.

Self-Care Techniques

In the midst of anger and bargaining, self-care emerges as a lifeline to soothe the turbulent waters of emotion. It is not a luxury but a necessity, a science-proven means of restoring balance to your mind and body. Let's explore them in detail.

Mindfulness is the practice of intentionally focusing your attention on the present moment, without judgment. It involves observing your thoughts, emotions, and bodily sensations without attempting to change them. This practice has been extensively researched and has shown significant benefits for mental and emotional well-being.

Studies have found that its regular practice can reduce symptoms of anxiety and depression, and also improve attention and cognitive functioning (Hofmann et al., 2010; Tang et al., 2015).

To start practicing mindfulness, you can follow the next guide, but feel free to research online or seek professional guidance:

1. Find a quiet space where you can sit or lie down comfortably.
2. Close your eyes and take a moment to center yourself.
3. Begin by focusing your attention on your breath. Notice the sensation of each inhale and exhale.
4. If your mind starts to wander, gently bring your focus back to your breath without judgment.
5. Start with just a few minutes a day and gradually increase the duration as you become more comfortable.

Relaxation techniques have proven to be effective in reducing stress and promoting relaxation. They encompass a variety of practices specifically designed for these purposes. One common technique is deep breathing, where you take slow, deep breaths to activate the body's relaxation response. This can lower heart rate and reduce the production of stress hormones (Ma et al., 2017).

Progressive muscle relaxation is another technique that involves tensing and then relaxing different muscle groups in your body. This can alleviate physical tension and promote a sense of calm. To begin, find a quiet space, sit or lie down, and focus on your breath.

1. Choose a quiet and peaceful environment to practice.
2. Sit or lie down in a comfortable position.
3. Start with deep breathing: Inhale slowly through your nose for a count of four, hold your breath for four, and exhale through your mouth for four.
4. Repeat this deep breathing pattern for a few minutes, allowing your body to relax with each breath.
5. For progressive muscle relaxation, begin by tensing a muscle group (e.g., your hand) for 5 seconds and then release. Move through different muscle groups, working your way from head to toe.

Another thing you can do is engage in joyful activities. These activities will obviously vary from one person to another, but they all share a common goal: to nourish your soul and uplift your spirits. Participating in hobbies, spending time in nature, or connecting with loved ones can all fall into this category.

Scientifically, engaging in activities that bring joy has been linked to the release of dopamine, a neurotransmitter associated with pleasure and reward (Kringelbach & Berridge, 2009). Such activities can also reduce levels of stress hormones like cortisol (Garner et al., 2011).

To begin incorporating joyful activities into your life, take a moment to reflect on what truly brings you happiness. Make a list of these activities and commit to setting aside time for them regularly. Whether it's reading a book, painting, hiking, or simply spending quality time with loved ones, prioritize activities that rejuvenate your spirit.

Incorporating these self-care practices into your daily routine can have a profound impact on your emotional well-being. Remember that self-care is not a luxury; it's a necessity for maintaining balance and resilience in the face of life's challenges. As you embark on this journey, approach these practices with an open heart and a willingness to nurture your inner self.

With newfound awareness and resilience, I invite you to turn the page and venture into the next chapter, where we will unravel further insights and strategies to navigate the complex terrain of the depression stage.

Make Abandonment Recovery a Daily Practice with This 30-Day Challenge

To make this step in your healing journey more manageable, I've created a 30-Day Self-Care Challenge just for you!

These small, meaningful actions can help you rebuild a stronger, more compassionate relationship with yourself. Whether it's a grounding exercise, a moment of reflection, or a simple act of kindness toward yourself, these practices will help you heal and move forward, one day at a time.

Download your workbook now by visiting: https://booksforbetterlife.com/abandonment-recovery or scan the QR code:

6

Navigating the Depths of Depression

"Birds never know if the sun will rise, yet they sing every day right before dawn. And sure enough, the sun emerges, defeating the most ominous mourn. Be the herald of impossible light, even amidst the worries of souls most weary. The darkness of the world may not be your fault, to light up the world is your existential duty."

— Abhijit Naskar

In the stillness of the night, when the world sleeps under the dark blanket sprinkled with stars, our minds often wander into the depths of contemplation. In these moments, we may find ourselves pondering the enigmatic nature of life, with its peaks of joy and valleys of despair. It's during these moments of reflection that we recognize the enduring truth—much like the birds who serenade the dawn without certainty of its arrival, we too must persist in our quest for light, even amidst the darkest of nights.

Together, we shall embark on a journey through the shadowy recesses of the human psyche, where darkness often threatens to engulf the flickering flames of hope. We may uncover the emotional chasms that define depression, examining its far-reaching impact on our mental and physical well-being. Through the lens of science and the crucible of personal experience, we shall seek to understand the contours of this mysterious stage in the healing process.

I'll share with you the tales of those I've encountered in my practice, individuals who, like birds at twilight, have grappled with the uncertainty of dawn. Their stories are a testament to the indomitable human spirit, and their resilience shines as a beacon of hope through the darkest of nights.

In the predawn stillness of our lives, we often find ourselves questioning the arrival of the sun. In those moments of uncertainty, we can learn a profound lesson from the birds. They never know with absolute certainty if the sun will rise, yet they sing each morning, heralding the possibility of light. This unwavering faith in the dawn, even amidst the darkest nights, mirrors the resilience that resides within each of us. Depression, however, can obscure that inner light, casting shadows of despair and isolation. Yet, it's precisely in these moments when we must strive to become the heralds of impossible light.

Depression is a heavy, intricate net of emotions; it envelops people, leaving them feeling lost in the labyrinth of their minds. It's a condition that's far from rare in today's world, affecting around 280 million people across the globe (World Health

Organization, 2023). But beyond the statistics, depression is a deeply personal experience, a journey through the darkest corners of one's emotional landscape.

At its core, this disorder is a profound response to life's challenges, a spectrum of emotions that range from persistent sadness to profound despair. It's a condition that transcends mere feelings of unhappiness; it engulfs individuals in a thick fog of hopelessness. For those who've never traversed its depths, it can be challenging to grasp the emotional weight that depression carries.

Depression doesn't just exist in the realm of emotions; it has a physical and psychological footprint. Those grappling with despair and deep sadness may find themselves trapped in a cycle of self-doubt, guilt, and self-criticism. The simplest of tasks can become insurmountable obstacles, draining their energy and motivation. Sleep disturbances, appetite changes, and unexplained physical pains often accompany the emotional turmoil, adding to the overall burden (Trivedi, 2004).

Scientific research has provided valuable insights into the emotional experiences associated with depression. Studies have revealed alterations in brain chemistry, particularly involving neurotransmitters like serotonin, norepinephrine, and dopamine. These imbalances contribute to the emotional landscape of depression, amplifying feelings of sadness, despair, and disconnection (Trivedi, 2004; Greden, 2003).

Yet, amid the clinical descriptions and statistics; for those facing it, the emotional affairs are overwhelming.

Life often presents us with challenging chapters filled with abandonment, loss, and heartbreak. These experiences, while universal, can be particularly potent triggers for depressive episodes. The emotional toll of abandonment, the profound sense of loss, and the agony of heartbreak can sow the seeds of depression.

Grief plays a pivotal role in understanding this connection. When we lose someone or something dear to us, whether through death, the dissolution of a relationship, or the shattering of our dreams, we enter a mourning process. This process involves various emotional stages, which can be remarkably similar to the stages of depression. The deep sadness, the sense of emptiness, and the feelings of isolation are familiar to anyone who has experienced either depression or profound loss.

Research consistently supports this connection. Studies have shown that individuals who have experienced significant life events, especially those involving loss, are at a higher risk of developing depression (Monroe et al., 1999). It underscores the complex relationship between our emotional traumas and the onset of this challenging condition.

Thanks to my profession, I've had the opportunity to walk alongside countless individuals on their process through the depths of depression. These journeys have shaped my understanding of the human spirit's resilience in the face of darkness. It's through these experiences that I've witnessed the transformative power of empathy, compassion, and therapeutic support.

A Story

One story in particular comes to mind; the one of a 15-year-old survivor of trafficking, etched a profound and lasting impression upon me, transcending the boundaries of my role as a therapist. It was a stark reminder that depression is not merely a psychological condition but an immersive and encompassing experience that permeates every facet of a person's life.

I remember the moment when I first met her. The deep-seated sorrow in her eyes mirrored the immense pain and suffering she had endured. It was difficult to fathom how a young girl could bear witness to such hostility and violence, yet possess an unwavering resolve to survive. Her courage was a testament to the incredible strength that resides within us, even when faced with the darkest of circumstances.

That little—but enormous—girl taught me invaluable lessons about the human spirit, resilience, and the capacity to endure, lessons that transcended the boundaries of our roles.

With time, I watched her transform. Her once-heavy burden of despair gradually lifted, and she emerged as a beacon of hope. Today, when I see her in her pediatrician's uniform, her smile radiating warmth and optimism, I am reminded that life, despite its relentless challenges, has the power to rise from even the heaviest of rubble.

Her example underscores a vital truth: Depression is not a reflection of who we are but rather an expression of our pain and life experiences. It is an inner monster that we confront, a part of our narrative, but it does not define our entirety. She, like all of us, is infinitely more than her inner struggles, and her story serves as a powerful testament to the resilience of the human spirit.

The Healing Power of Grief

In our society, there exists a prevailing tendency to suppress grief, often driven by discomfort with facing the depths of our emotions. We're often told to be strong, to move on, or that time will heal all wounds. However, this societal pressure to repress anguish does have detrimental effects on our mental health.

Allowing oneself to grieve is not a sign of weakness; it's a crucial and necessary step in the healing process. Grief is the natural response to loss, and when we deny ourselves the opportunity to grieve, we deny ourselves the chance to heal.

We might busy ourselves with work, drown our sorrows in distractions, or simply put on a brave face and soldier on. While this may seem like resilience, it can lead to a different kind of suffering—one that festers beneath the surface, invisible but potent.

Grieving means acknowledging the pain, sadness, and loss that are an inevitable part of the human experience. By doing so, we create a safe space to process our emotions and begin the journey toward healing.

Psychologically, allowing grief has profound benefits. It

helps reduce the emotional burden that accumulates when we suppress our feelings. When we acknowledge our pain, we lighten the load we carry, making room for resilience to flourish. Studies in psychology have consistently shown that suppressing grief can lead to prolonged suffering and even manifest as physical ailments (O'Connor, 2019).

This natural and essential emotional process is a testament to the love and connection we feel for what we've lost. Kübler-Ross described the previously covered stages of grief. She empathized that these stages are not linear, nor does everyone experience them all. However, they provide a framework for understanding how individuals process grief.

Grief, in essence, is a process of making sense of our experiences and integrating them into our life story. It's a way of honoring what has been lost and finding meaning in the midst of pain.

Real-life stories abound around us, illustrating the immense power of grief. Individuals who have traversed the terrain of grief often emerge with newfound resilience and wisdom. Grief allowed them to channel it into personal growth. This is the essence of grief as a fundamental emotional process—it allows us to transform our sorrow into resilience.

Grief, when faced with courage and self-compassion, has the potential to lead us to greater self-awareness, resilience, and emotional maturity. It becomes a catalyst for personal growth, a force that propels us forward rather than holding us back.

We have previously highlighted the role that self-compassion plays when navigating grief—and we will come back to it later. It involves treating ourselves with the same kindness and understanding that we would offer a dear friend. It means acknowledging our pain without judgment and allowing ourselves to grieve without self-blame.

In the following pages, we will explore practical strategies for cultivating self-compassion, communication approaches, and seeking professional guidance in your healing journey.

Strategies for Seeking Support and Connection

One of the foundational pillars of navigating depression is open and honest communication with trusted friends and family members. Yet, this simple concept can often be challenging, as depression can shroud our ability to convey our needs effectively.

It's essential to understand the common barriers that individuals with depression may face when trying to communicate. Stigma, shame, or the fear of burdening loved ones can act as formidable obstacles. However, these barriers can be overcome.

Practical tips and techniques can pave the way for meaningful conversations. By expressing your emotional needs, you allow others to understand and support you better. It's not a sign of weakness but an act of self-compassion.

Consider a scenario where someone struggles with depression. They had always been the pillar of strength for their family, and the thought of revealing their vulnerability was daunting. But when they mustered the courage to speak with their spouse, explaining their emotional turmoil, they found an unexpected wellspring of support.

Empathy and active listening are essential components of fostering meaningful connections within personal relationships. It's not just about speaking but also about hearing and understanding.

I've witnessed firsthand the power of professional guidance in my patients' lives. Depression, a seemingly insurmountable mountain, can be scaled with the right support. Sometimes, the perspective and tools a therapist provides can make all the difference.

Therapeutic Techniques

In mental health, the techniques and approaches to treat a specific situation are very diverse; as diverse as the problems, challenges, and people that present themselves in each therapeutic office around the world every day. Misconceptions or hesitations about therapy are common. Some may question its value or worry about the stigma attached to it. So, let's analyze in detail their perspective, scientific background, and practical approaches.

Cognitive-behavioral therapy (CBT) is one of the most well-researched and evidence-based therapeutic approaches for depression. Its foundation lies in the understanding of how thoughts, emotions, and behaviors are interconnected. Research studies have consistently shown that CBT can lead to significant improvements in depressive symptoms (Hofmann et al., 2012).

This approach operates on the principle that changing negative thought patterns and replacing them with more adaptive ones can alleviate depression. Studies using neuroimaging techniques have consistently demonstrated the positive impact of CBT on brain activity, particularly in areas associated with emotional regulation (Bomyea et al., 2020).

Interpersonal therapy (IPT) is another well-researched method; it focuses on improving interpersonal relationships and communication as a means to alleviate depressive symptoms. Scientific research supports the idea that social support and relationships play a crucial role in mental well-being. Studies have shown that IPT can effectively reduce depression symptoms by addressing interpersonal issues (Umberson & Karas Montez, 2010).

Then, in the field of psychotherapies, we encounter many mindfulness-based approaches, such as mindfulness-based stress reduction and mindfulness-based cognitive therapy (MBCT). These are drawn from contemplative traditions and modern psychology. Scientific studies have shown that mindfulness practices can lead to changes in brain structure and function (Hölzel et al., 2011).

For example, research using MRI has indicated that regular mindfulness meditation can increase the density of gray matter in brain regions associated with memory, self-awareness, and compassion. These structural changes align with the observed improvements in depression symptoms among individuals who engage in mindfulness practices (Hölzel et al., 2011).

Psychodynamic therapy, with its roots in psychoanalysis, delves into the unconscious processes that influence our thoughts and behaviors. While it may not rely on neuroimaging studies as heavily as other approaches, it still holds scientific validity.

Another approach you can consider is acceptance and commitment therapy (ACT). It is grounded in the science of behavioral analysis and functional contextualism. It combines aspects of CBT with mindfulness practices. Studies have shown that ACT can lead to significant reductions in depressive symptoms (Rauwenhoff et al., 2022).

ACT's focus on values clarification and committed action aligns with research on goal-setting and motivation. Scientific evidence supports the idea that aligning one's actions with personal values can enhance well-being and psychological flexibility (Rauwenhoff et al., 2022).

Keep in mind that these therapeutic approaches are not universal solutions. A good professional needs to adapt them to your particular situation and needs. Also, these methods are not mutually exclusive; they can be integrated to create tailored treatments for individuals. The beauty of science-based therapy is that it continually evolves, adapting to new research findings and insights.

To address a problem as large and important as depression, it is necessary to adopt measures on all fronts: nurturing your physical wellness, seeking comfort and support from health professionals when necessary, researching, and, of course, not neglecting your loved ones, and asking them to accompany you in your process. Many times, we can feel that we are a nuisance or a burden to those around us, so we tend to isolate ourselves and not share our experiences with others.

Addressing something as complex as depression can feel overwhelming, but you don't have to go through it alone. It's like tackling a big challenge that requires a team effort. So, here's a friendly suggestion: Consider having a heart-to-heart chat with someone you trust, like a friend or family member. Let them in on what's been going on with you. You might think it's a lot to ask, but trust me, they care about you more than you realize.

Sometimes, we hesitate because we worry about becoming a burden. I get it, we all have those thoughts sometimes. But here's the thing: Isolation can make things tougher, especially when dealing with depression, anxiety, and other mental health affairs. So, instead of trying to be the lone superhero, think about how your trusted person can be your sidekick in this journey.

It could be as simple as them being there to listen when you need to vent, or maybe accompanying you on a walk. Even helping with everyday stuff when you're not up to it. You see, asking for support is actually a pretty brave move.

Asking for company and support for our loved ones is

paramount. Yet, you may still feel like they don't fully understand your feelings. In this scenario, support groups and communities offer a lifeline—a sense of belonging and shared understanding that can combat the pervasive feeling of being alone in one's struggles.

These networks come in various forms, from in-person meetings to online forums. They cater to diverse needs and interests. For example, some individuals may find comfort in talking to peers who share similar experiences, while others might benefit from the guidance of mental health professionals within support groups.

Support networks are not just about seeking help; they're about connecting with others who truly understand. They provide a space where you can express your feelings without judgment.

Actively engaging with support networks is key. Whether it's attending meetings or participating in online communities—blogs, video blogs, Facebook groups, and so on, reaching out is a necessary step toward healing.

Start with 22 CBT Worksheets to Conquer Negative Thoughts Today!

*To help you on your path to mental well-being, I've created **22 CBT Worksheets**—practical guides filled with exercises and strategies rooted in Cognitive Behavioral Therapy.*

These sheets are designed to help you challenge negative thought patterns, reframe your mindset, and create lasting emotional resilience. Think of it as a hands-on tool to support you in taking small yet meaningful steps toward a healthier, more positive outlook on life.

Get immediate access to your workbook by visiting: https://booksforbetterlife.com/abandonment-recovery or scan the QR code now:

7

Finding Healing in Acceptance

"A moment of hate can devastate a lifetime of work, whereas a moment of love can break barriers that took a lifetime to build."

— Nelson Mandela

Acceptance, in the realm of mental health recovery, is the pivotal point where healing begins to gain momentum. It's the acknowledgment that our emotional experiences, no matter how painful or uncomfortable, are a part of our reality. This acknowledgment is not passive resignation; rather, it's a profound and active process of facing our emotions head-on.

Psychological theories and frameworks, such as the aforementioned ACT and MBCT, underscore the significance of acceptance in mental health recovery. These approaches emphasize that resisting or avoiding our emotions often leads to prolonged suffering. Instead, embracing our feelings—no matter how distressing—can be a catalyst for transformation.

At the core of acceptance lies the power to acknowledge our pain and suffering without judgment. It pushes us to release the resistance that often exacerbates emotional distress. This resistance manifests when we try to deny or suppress our feelings, believing that they are undesirable or unwelcome. Yet, it only intensifies our suffering. Like a rope tangled in your hand that you refuse to let go hurts you, only when we face acceptance, with its vertigo, can we find relief.

What happens when we avoid confronting our emotions? Well, they tend to linger beneath the surface, like a persistent storm cloud. Acceptance, on the other hand, is the gentle rain that allows these emotions to be acknowledged, felt, and eventually transformed.

Practical techniques and exercises are usually useful for people to practice acceptance in their daily lives. These may include mindfulness meditation, or journaling to express and process their feelings. The following are some practical strategies to strengthen our acceptance abilities:

- **Become aware of your resistance:** Begin by recognizing when you're resisting your emotions or experiences. This resistance often operates on autopilot, so making a conscious effort to notice it is the first crucial step toward change.

- **Explore the roots of resistance:** Delve deeper into your resistance patterns by examining their origins. Consider how your childhood experiences and the responses of adults around you may have shaped your current ways of handling emotions. Writing down these reflections can provide insight into your habitual patterns and foster self-acceptance.

- **Connect with your inner child:** Imagine yourself as a vulnerable child to develop self-compassion. We often criticize ourselves more harshly than we would others. Visualizing your inner child can soften self-judgment and make it easier to show understanding when facing difficult emotions.

To do this, find a quiet and comfortable space where you won't be disturbed. Close your eyes and take a few deep breaths, allowing your body to relax. Picture a specific moment from your childhood where you felt safe and happy. It could be playing in a park, sitting in your favorite spot at home, or any memory that brings a sense of warmth.

As you visualize, pay attention to the details: the colors, sounds, and even the smells associated with that memory. Engage your senses fully. Now, imagine yourself as the child in that scene. See the clothes you're wearing, notice your expressions, and feel the joy or innocence that radiates from that younger version of yourself.

To deepen the connection, you can also engage in a dialogue. Ask your inner child what they need or how they feel. Provide comfort and reassurance, just as you would to a real child. This interactive visualization can foster a profound sense of self-compassion, making it easier to extend kindness and understanding to yourself, especially when confronting challenging emotions.

- **Consistent practice:** Cultivating acceptance is a skill that requires regular practice. Like any habit, it becomes more natural with repetition. When confronted with challenging emotions, consciously choose acceptance as a mental habit. Over time, these choices will become ingrained, and acceptance will become a more effortless response. Here's a simple practice to get you started:

1. **Mindful Awareness:** Begin by bringing your awareness to the present moment. Notice the thoughts and emotions that arise without judgment. Be an observer of your inner experience.

2. **Nonjudgmental Observation:** As you observe your thoughts and emotions, practice nonjudgmental awareness. Resist the urge to label them as 'good' or 'bad.' Instead, acknowledge them as part of your present experience.

3. **Choosing Acceptance:** When faced with difficult emotions, consciously choose acceptance. Remind yourself that it's okay to feel the way you do. Embrace the idea that all emotions are valid and temporary.

4. **Self-Compassion:** Extend self-compassion to yourself. Treat yourself with the kindness you would offer to a friend facing a similar situation. Understand that, like

everyone else, you are navigating the complexities of human emotions.

5. **Repeat and Reinforce:** Repeat this practice regularly. The more you consciously choose acceptance, the more it becomes ingrained in your thought patterns. With time and repetition, acceptance will evolve into a more effortless and instinctive response to challenging emotions."

As I mentioned before, I've accompanied innumerable people through the labyrinth of depression. Time and again, I've observed how the stage of acceptance becomes a definitive turning point, a rebirth of sorts, where individuals begin to experience a profound sense of relief and peace.

Before reaching this stage, many of my patients grapple with relentless sadness, loneliness, and despair. Depression can feel like an unending storm, where every day is shrouded in darkness. The weight of emotional pain seems insurmountable, and hope often remains elusive.

However, as we go deeper into the process of acceptance, something extraordinary begins to happen. It's as though a long-lost key has been found, unlocking the door to a new dimension of healing: Patients start to understand that acceptance is not about erasing pain or pretending it doesn't exist. Instead, it's about facing pain with courage and compassion; to stop avoiding pain, allow themselves to feel it, and go through it to finally change their skin.

For those who have been in the throes of depression, this

realization is revolutionary. They learn that acknowledging their emotions—no matter how painful or challenging—is not a sign of weakness but an act of profound strength. It's a recognition that they are not defined by their depression; they are individuals who have the capacity to navigate their emotional landscape.

As the therapeutic journey progresses, patients gradually release the resistance that has been holding them captive. They let go of the belief that they should be free of pain and suffering, and instead, they embrace their emotional reality. This shift from resistance to acceptance is akin to shedding a heavy burden.

Through various therapeutic techniques, including all of those presented in this guide, we can learn to sit with our emotions without judgment. For example, one mindfulness practice that is broadly used in psychology to foster acceptance is the body scan technique. You just need to take a few minutes each day to focus your attention on different parts of your body, starting from your toes and moving up to your head. This practice encourages you to notice any physical sensations without trying to change them, promoting a sense of acceptance.

Journaling is always useful for this purpose. Try these prompts to explore and embrace your feelings of acceptance:

- Write about a recent situation where you found it difficult to accept something. What were your initial emotions, and how did they change as you reflected on it?

- Describe an experience where you felt truly at peace with yourself and your circumstances. What contributed to this sense of acceptance?

- List three things you appreciate about yourself, even if they relate to your journey in overcoming challenges.

Writing a letter for yourself is a gentle and effective way to find self-compassion and cultivate a deeper and more benevolent bond with yourself. Write as if you were corresponding to a dear friend who's struggling with the same situation. Be kind, and understanding, and offer words of support and encouragement. Reading this letter aloud can be a powerful way to cultivate self-compassion and acceptance.

A lot of people at the height of their depression could barely find the energy to get out of bed and transform into individuals with a renewed sense of purpose. They begin to see their depression not as an enemy but as a part of their life journey. It becomes a teacher, offering lessons in resilience, empathy, and the depth of the human experience.

The relief that comes with acceptance is palpable. Patients describe a sense of unburdening, as though they've finally set down a heavy load they've been carrying for far too long. The storm clouds of depression begin to dissipate, allowing rays of hope to break through.

In essence, the acceptance stage marks a definitive rebirth for my patients. It's a moment where they shed the skin of their old selves—defined by suffering—and step into the light of a new understanding. They emerge as warriors who have faced their inner demons and found peace within.

Nurturing Self-Love and Self-Acceptance

Imagine self-acceptance as the soil in which the seeds of self-love are planted. It's the act of acknowledging and embracing oneself, warts and all, without harsh judgment or self-condemnation; it's about making peace with our flaws and imperfections, remembering that they are an inherent part of our humanity.

Self-love, on the other hand, is the blossoming of this self-acceptance. It's the gentle embrace we offer to our own hearts, a declaration of worthiness, and an affirmation of our intrinsic value. Together, self-acceptance and self-love form a symbiotic relationship, each reinforcing the other.

Research in psychology consistently highlights the profound impact of self-acceptance and self-love on mental health. Studies have shown that individuals who practice self-acceptance tend to experience lower levels of anxiety, depression, and psychological distress. They are more resilient in the face of life's challenges, as they don't internalize setbacks as reflections of their worth (Zhang et al., 2022).

One of the most beautiful aspects of this interconnectedness is that it's accessible to everyone, regardless of their current emotional state. Whether you're in the depths of depression or on the path to recovery, the journey of self-acceptance and self-love is open to you.

Self-compassion acts as a gentle guide on the path to self-acceptance. It's the practice of treating ourselves with the same kindness and understanding that we would extend to a dear friend in times of struggle. It allows us to recognize our suffering without judgment and offer ourselves some soothe and comfort. Besides, it provides a lifeline in moments of despair, a reminder that we are deserving of love and care, even when we feel at our lowest.

I've witnessed patients undergo remarkable transformations through the cultivation of self-compassion. They learn to befriend their inner critic, replacing self-criticism with self-kindness. This shift doesn't happen overnight, but as they practice self-compassion, they begin to see themselves through a more empathetic lens.

Nurturing self-love is a paramount step to achieving these abilities of looking at ourselves with compassion and love, and it requires active participation. Here are some exercises and practices that can guide you in developing a loving relationship with yourself:

- **Self-reflection**: Take moments to reflect on your strengths, values, and unique qualities. Write down what makes you special and deserving of love.

- **Self-affirmations**: Create positive affirmations that resonate with you. Let me give you some examples:

1. *I am worthy of love and acceptance just as I am.*
2. *I am resilient, and I can overcome any challenge that comes*

my way.
3. *I am not defined by my past; I am free to create my future.*
4. *I have the strength to face adversity with grace and courage.*
5. *I treat myself with kindness and compassion, just as I would a dear friend.*

Feel free to choose or adapt these affirmations to resonate with your personal experiences and needs. The key is to make them genuinely meaningful to you, so they have a powerful impact on you. Repeat them daily to counter negative self-talk.

- **Self-appreciation letters:** Write letters to yourself, expressing gratitude and appreciation for who you are. Treat yourself as you would a dear friend.

- **Self-care rituals:** Establish self-care routines that prioritize your well-being. Whether it's a warm bath, a walk in nature, or meditation, these acts of self-kindness can be transformative.

- **Mindful self-compassion:** Practice mindfulness and self-compassion exercises regularly. They can help you navigate difficult emotions with kindness and understanding.

The route to self-love is unique for each of us, and it's perfectly okay to take it one step at a time. Be patient with yourself, and know that you are deserving of the love and acceptance you offer to others.

Access Emotional Comfort Wherever You Are with Powerful Grief, Loss, and Heartbreak Affirmation Cards

Throughout this book, we've touched on the power of affirmations as a tool for healing and self-compassion. To help you integrate this practice simply into your journey, I've created these Affirmation Cards—a collection of heartfelt reminders designed to support you through your most difficult moments anytime, anywhere!

Each card is crafted to bring comfort, encourage self-kindness, and remind you that healing is a journey, not a destination. Whether you use them to start your day, as a moment of reflection, or whenever the weight feels heavy, these cards are here to offer a guiding light through the darkness.

Get immediate access to your affirmations cards by visiting: https://booksforbetterlife.com/abandonment-recovery or scan the QR code now:

You are not alone in this. Let these affirmations remind

you of your strength and your ability to heal, one step at a time.

Exploring New Paths

Psychologically speaking, acceptance allows us to break free from the shackles of our past pain and limitations. It creates space within us, providing room for fresh opportunities and unexplored potential. Rather than being trapped in the past, we become open to the richness of the present and the possibilities of the future.

Carl Rogers' person-centered therapy is a remarkable theory, which emphasizes the importance of self-acceptance in personal growth. Rogers believed that when individuals fully accept themselves, including their flaws and imperfections, they experience greater congruence, self-actualization, and overall well-being (O'Hara, 1989).

At the heart of Rogers' theory is the belief in the inherent goodness and potential for growth within each individual. He proposed that, given the right conditions, people naturally tend to move toward self-actualization, a state of becoming the best version of themselves.

He introduced the concept of self-concept, which is how individuals perceive themselves. This self-concept is composed of three components: self-image, (how we see ourselves), self-esteem (the value and worth we assign to ourselves), and ideal self (the person we aspire to become).

From this basis, Rogers emphasized the importance of congruence, which is the alignment between an individual's self-concept and their actual experiences. When there is congruence, individuals have a more accurate and realistic view of themselves, which fosters personal growth.

He also identified how society often imposes conditions of worth on individuals. These conditions dictate that people are only worthy of love and acceptance if they meet certain criteria, such as success, beauty, or conforming to societal norms. This can lead to incongruence, as individuals may develop a self-concept based on these external conditions rather than their authentic selves.

So, how does all of this relate to self-acceptance?

Self-Acceptance and Congruence

In Rogers' view, self-acceptance is a pivotal aspect of congruence and personal growth. When individuals fully accept themselves, including their flaws and imperfections, they move closer to congruence. This means that their self-concept aligns more closely with their actual experiences and feelings.

For example, if someone struggles with depression, self-acceptance involves acknowledging and accepting their feelings of sadness and despair without judgment. They recognize that these feelings are a part of their current reality, but they do not define their entire identity.

When we put in practice this approach, we experience greater congruence, which Rogers believed to be a fundamental condition for personal growth and self-actualization. In other words, by accepting ourselves and our background, we can move forward in our personal development journey. These are some of the things you can do to foster self-acceptance:

- **Self-reflection journal:** Start by keeping a self-reflection journal. Dedicate some time each day to write about your thoughts, feelings, and experiences. This journal will become a safe space for you to explore your self-concept and any conditions of worth that may have influenced it.

- **Three components of self-concept:** Break down your self-concept into its three components: self-image, self-esteem, and ideal self. Take time to write down your perceptions of each. What do you see when you visualize yourself? How do you value yourself? Who is the person you aspire to become? Reflecting on these aspects can provide clarity about your self-concept.

- **Conditions of worth:** Examine your life and identify any conditions of worth that may have been imposed on you by society, family, or cultural influences. Make a list of these conditions and reflect on how they have influenced your self-concept. Are there aspects of yourself that you've suppressed or denied due to these conditions?

Acceptance, in this context, becomes the cornerstone of personal development. It's the recognition that we don't have to be defined by our past or our pain. Instead, it offers the potential for a life unburdened by the weight of unresolved emotions.

Once we've embraced acceptance, we're better equipped to envision a future beyond our current pain. It's a future where healing becomes the fertile ground for personal development and fulfillment. To embark on this journey, it's essential to set a clear vision for our future selves.

Setting realistic and inspiring goals is a crucial aspect of this process. When we can clearly visualize our desired future, it becomes a powerful motivator for personal growth. This visualization isn't limited to external achievements; it extends to our emotional and psychological well-being.

Consider the concept of post-traumatic growth, which highlights how individuals can emerge from adversity with newfound strengths and perspectives. Through acceptance, we can harness the lessons learned from our pain and channel them into personal growth. It's akin to using the debris of a storm to build a stronger foundation.

This is a science-backed thing: Studies show that individuals who have experienced significant adversity and trauma often report a greater appreciation for life, enhanced personal strength, and a deeper sense of meaning (Jayawickreme & Blackie, 2014). These outcomes are not merely the absence of pain but the presence of profound personal growth.

Creating a Foundation

As we previously covered, acceptance is like the bedrock of a resilient psyche. It's the sturdy foundation upon which we can build emotional strength. Think of it as the stable ground that allows us to weather life's storms.

Embracing our emotions and experiences through acceptance enables us to respond to adversity in a healthier way. It allows us to bounce back from life's challenges with greater strength and resilience.

The aforementioned concept of post-traumatic growth comes into play here. To refresh, this concept states that through acceptance, we can facilitate personal development even in the aftermath of difficult experiences. It's not about denying or avoiding the pain; it's about embracing it and emerging stronger.

Think of it as a tree in a storm. The tree doesn't resist the wind; instead, it allows the wind to pass through its branches. In doing so, it remains standing tall. In much the same way, when we accept the turbulence of our emotions and experiences, we become emotionally stable.

Now, let's explore practical strategies for integrating acceptance into our daily lives. This integration is key to enhancing emotional well-being and resilience.

Mindfulness exercises are an excellent starting point. They help us become more aware of our emotional responses. This practice allows us to observe our emotions, which makes self-acceptance more accessible.

Cultivating a growth mindset is another powerful strategy. This perspective encourages us to view challenges as opportunities for learning and development. It's the belief that we can grow through adversity. This allows us to be more likely to accept our experiences rather than resist them. *How can I do this?* you may be wondering. Here, you have some ideas:

- **Reframe challenges:** When confronted with a difficulty, consciously reframe your perspective. Instead of seeing it as an obstacle, view it as a chance to learn and develop. Ask yourself, *What can I gain from this experience?* This shift in mindset can make challenges feel less daunting.

- **Embrace mistakes:** Recognize that making mistakes is a natural part of growth. Instead of criticizing yourself for errors, use them as opportunities to improve. Reflect on what you've learned from your mistakes and how you can apply those lessons moving forward.

- **Set growth-oriented goals:** Define goals that align with personal growth and development. These goals should challenge you to step out of your comfort zone and acquire new skills or knowledge. As you work toward these objectives, you'll naturally adopt a growth mindset.

- **Challenge negative self-talk:** Pay attention to your inner dialogue. If you catch yourself engaging in self-limiting or self-critical thoughts, challenge them. Replace negative self-talk with affirmations that reinforce your ability to learn and grow.

- **Seek feedback:** Welcome constructive feedback from others. Feedback provides valuable insights into areas where you can improve. Instead of feeling defensive, use feedback as a tool for personal development.

- **Practice patience:** Understand that personal growth takes time. Be patient with yourself and acknowledge that setbacks are a part of the journey. It's okay to experience moments of frustration or doubt; what matters is your commitment to growth.

Of course, self-care practices are crucial. Adequate sleep, regular exercise, and a balanced diet contribute significantly to emotional resilience. When our bodies are nourished and rested, we're better equipped to handle life's challenges.

For a good sleeping pattern, consider:

- Aim for 7–9 hours of quality sleep per night. The exact amount varies from person to person, but this range is generally recommended for adults.
- Create a consistent sleep schedule by going to bed and waking up at the same times every day, even on weekends. This helps regulate your body's internal clock.
- Prioritize sleep hygiene. Keep your bedroom cool, dark, and quiet. Remove electronic devices that emit blue light, as it can interfere with sleep.
- Limit caffeine and alcohol intake, especially in the evening, as these substances can disrupt sleep patterns.
- Avoid heavy meals close to bedtime and reduce fluid intake before sleep to prevent nighttime awakenings.
- Engage in relaxation techniques such as reading, listening to calm music, deep breathing, or meditation before

bedtime to calm the mind and promote better sleep.

When it comes to alimentation, keep in mind the following:

- A balanced diet includes a variety of foods from different food groups to ensure you receive essential nutrients including proteins, minerals, vitamins, and amino acids, among other paramount compounds.
- Focus on whole foods such as fruits, vegetables, whole grains, lean proteins, and healthy fats.
- Limit processed and sugary foods, as they can lead to energy spikes and crashes.
- Stay hydrated by drinking plenty of water throughout the day. Between 2 and 3 liters is enough, depending on your body characteristics and activities.
- Pay attention to portion sizes to avoid overeating. Eating in moderation is key to maintaining a balanced diet and avoiding stress peaks derived from hormonal changes.
- Consider consulting a registered dietitian for personalized dietary guidance based on your individual needs and goals, since your specific caloric intake and nutritional needs depend on plenty of individual and contextual factors.

As we move forward, may we do so with our heads held high, our hearts wide open, and the knowledge that through acceptance, we become the architects of our own flourishing.

8

Building Emotional Resilience Beyond Healing

"My barn having burned down, I can now see the moon."

— Mizuta Masahide

We've traveled through the storms of emotions, navigated the labyrinth of healing, and emerged on the other side, wiser and stronger. This chapter marks a moment of celebration, a recognition of your unwavering commitment to healing and growth. Just as a burnt barn reveals the radiant moon, your journey through darkness has unveiled the brilliance of your resilience. Along the following pages, we explore the art of building emotional resilience beyond healing, transforming life's challenges into stepping stones toward a brighter future.

The psychological frameworks we have explored so far remind us that resilience is not a trait you either have or don't have; rather, it's a skill that you can cultivate and refine over time.

Just as muscles grow stronger with exercise, so does emotional resilience with practice. In this ongoing journey, you are the architect of your soundness, continuously shaping it through the choices you make and the lessons you learn.

Practical Steps for Nurturing Emotional Resilience

To nurture and strengthen your emotional resilience for the future, there are practical steps you can take. Self-reflection and self-awareness become allies in this endeavor. They enable you to delve deeper into your emotional responses and understand your unique coping mechanisms. Through this awareness, you can refine your strategies for handling adversity. Here, you can find some tips and ideas to put into practice:

- Engaging in creative activities like painting, drawing, or sculpting can provide insights into your emotions and thoughts. The act of creating art can be a form of self-expression and self-discovery.

- Conduct a body scan exercise where you focus your attention on each part of your body, starting from your toes and moving up to your head. Notice any physical sensations, tension, or discomfort. This can help you connect with your body's responses to emotions.

- Instead of traditional meditation, practice mindful walking. Take a slow, deliberate walk and pay close attention to the sensations in your feet as they touch the ground. Notice the rhythm of your steps and your surroundings.

- Dedicate a few minutes each day to check in with yourself. Ask questions like, *How am I feeling right now?* or, *What thoughts are on my mind?* Journaling these daily check-ins can provide valuable insights over time.

- Draw a simple map of your emotional landscape. Label different areas with emotions or states of mind. Reflect on where you currently stand on the map and why. This "emotional mapping" exercise can help you visualize your emotional experiences.

- Explore the connection between your physical sensations and emotions. When you notice tension or discomfort in your body, ask yourself what emotions or thoughts might be contributing to these sensations.

Building a support network is another crucial aspect of enhancing resilience. Cultivate relationships with friends, family, or mentors who provide guidance and encouragement during challenging times. They become your pillars of strength when life's storms arrive.

Resilience-Building Habits

Resilience-building habits, rooted in mindfulness, gratitude, and positive self-talk, also play a vital role. Practicing mindfulness keeps you attuned to the present moment, allowing you to navigate stressors with greater ease. Cultivating gratitude reminds you of life's blessings, even in difficult times. Positive self-talk acts as a guardian against self-doubt and negativity.

Some ways to practice these approaches are the following:

- In addition to the aforementioned conscious breathing and body scan techniques, you can also apply mindfulness in daily tasks such as cleaning yourself, eating, or doing housework. For **mindful eating**, pay full attention to your meals, savoring each bite. Notice the taste, texture, and aroma of your food. Eating mindfully can enhance your connection to your body and the present moment.

- Keep a gratitude journal where you write down three things you're grateful for each day. These can be small or significant moments. Reflect on why you appreciate them. You can write down something like: "Today, I'm grateful for the stunning sunrise I witnessed. The colors painted across the sky reminded me of the beauty in the world and filled me with a sense of awe."

- Take the time to **express gratitude** to the people in your life. Send a heartfelt thank-you message or note or simply tell someone you appreciate them and value their company and apport to your life.

- When you notice self-doubt or negative self-talk, **challenge those thoughts**. Ask yourself if they are based on facts or assumptions. Replace negative statements with positive, affirming ones. Let's say you have a thought like: *I'll never be good at public speaking. I always mess up and embarrass myself.* You could challenge it by asking yourself: *Is this based on facts or assumptions? Have there been times when I've successfully spoken in public and actually had an embarrassing* *situation? What were the factors?* Next, you can replace the first statement with something like this: *Public speaking is a skill I can improve with practice. I've delivered successful presentations in the past, and I'm capable of learning and growing in this area.*

- In your interactions with others, practice **active listening**. Focus on what the speaker is saying without judgment or forming responses in your mind. This can deepen your connections and understanding.

Those with robust emotional resilience are better equipped to manage stress and maintain their mental health. Their emotional stability acts as a buffer against life's challenges, helping them stay grounded even when the world seems chaotic.

Scientific research reinforces the profound impact of resilience on both mental and physical health. It shows a reduced risk of mental health disorders, such as depression and anxiety, among individuals with strong emotional resilience. Additionally, resilience is associated with improved physical health outcomes, contributing to overall well-being (Charney, 2023).

This trait also enables people to tackle professional challenges with composure and creativity. Moreover, it fosters a sense of personal fulfillment and life satisfaction. Those who cultivate resilience tend to experience greater contentment and joy in their daily lives.

A Handy Toolkit

In our ongoing journey of well-being and resilience, it's essential to have some practical techniques and methods at your disposal. Think of this toolkit as a resource to turn to whenever you need support in maintaining your emotional balance. Here are some key strategies to keep in mind:

- **Mindfulness exercises:** Begin with mindfulness, a foundational practice that enhances self-awareness and helps reduce stress. Simple mindfulness exercises, like focused breathing or body scans, can be integrated into your daily routine.

- **Relaxation techniques:** Stress management is a vital part of emotional resilience. Try deep breathing exercises, progressive muscle relaxation, or even time management strategies to minimize stressors in your life.

- **Self-reflection practices:** Journaling is a powerful tool for self-reflection. It allows you to process your thoughts and emotions, gaining insight into your experiences. Consider setting aside time for journaling regularly.

- **Physical activity:** Don't underestimate the benefits of physical activity on your emotional well-being. Regular exercise can boost your mood, reduce stress, and improve brain dynamics, fostering mood stability.

Remember, the key is to have a variety of strategies at your disposal. What works best for you may vary depending on your current circumstances and emotional state. Personalize your toolkit to suit your preferences and needs.

Self-Care Support Strategies for Resilience

As you already know, self-care is a crucial aspect of maintaining emotional resilience. Here are some strategies tailored to support your resilience:

- As mentioned before, mindfulness is foundational. Consider incorporating mindfulness meditation into your routine. Apps and guided sessions are readily available to assist you in this practice.

- Stress is a part of life, but how you manage it can make all the difference. Deep breathing exercises, such as the 4-7-8 technique—inhale quietly through your nose for a count of four, hold your breath for a count of seven, and exhale audibly through your mouth for a count of eight—can help calm your nervous system. Progressive muscle relaxation is another effective method.

- Healthy coping mechanisms are vital. Journaling can help you process your emotions, seek clarity, and track your progress. Don't hesitate to lean on your support network when needed, whether through conversations or seeking professional help. Engaging in hobbies you enjoy can also provide a valuable emotional outlet.

To make these techniques a sustainable part of your daily life:

- **Design a self-care routine that suits your schedule and preferences.** Whether it's a morning mindfulness session, a midday walk, or an evening journaling practice, having a routine helps ensure consistency.

- **Consistency is key.** Regularly practicing these techniques strengthens their impact. Even on days when you don't feel particularly stressed or overwhelmed, maintaining your routine can help prevent future challenges.

- **Look to real-life examples of people around you who have successfully integrated self-care into their daily lives.** Their experiences can provide inspiration and guidance. You can also ask them for advice and share your progress with them.

- **Understand that self-care isn't a luxury; it's a necessity.** Prioritize your emotional well-being by making self-care an essential part of your daily routine. It's an investment in your long-term resilience and happiness.

A Tale About a Carrot, an Egg, and a Cup of Coffee

I have a story to tell you about resilience. It's a tale about a young woman who once found herself burdened by life's challenges. She reached a point where she felt overwhelmed, tired of the constant struggle, and considered giving up. It seemed that no matter how hard she fought, new problems would always arise.

One day, she turned to her mother, pouring out her heart about the difficulties she faced. She wondered how she could continue when it felt like the world was against her.

In response, her mother decided to impart a valuable lesson. She led her daughter to the kitchen and placed three pots filled with water on the stove. Soon, all three pots began to boil. Without uttering a word, her mother placed carrots in the first pot, eggs in the second, and ground coffee beans in the third. They simmered away as the young woman watched, perplexed.

After about 20 minutes, her mother turned off the burners. She carefully took out the carrots and put them in a bowl. She then retrieved the eggs and placed them in another bowl. Finally, she poured the brewed coffee into a third bowl.

Turning to her daughter, she asked a simple question, "Tell me, what do you see?"

The daughter replied, "I see carrots, eggs, and coffee, Mom."

Her mother invited her to examine each closely. She asked her to touch the carrots, and they were now soft. Then, her mother suggested cracking an egg. After removing the shell, they discovered the egg was hard-boiled. Finally, the daughter was encouraged to taste the coffee's rich aroma.

Perplexed but curious, the daughter inquired, "What does it all mean, Mom?"

With a gentle smile, her mother shared the profound lesson behind this seemingly mundane kitchen experiment. Each item—the carrots, eggs, and coffee beans—had faced the same adversity: boiling water. Yet, they responded differently, just as people do in the face of life's challenges.

The carrot, once unyielding, had softened and become weak. The egg, though fragile with a protective shell, had hardened on the inside. But the coffee beans had transformed the water itself. They had changed the circumstances they were placed in.

And so, her mother asked a poignant question, one that resonates with all of us when we confront adversity: "Which are you? When life's challenges boil around you, are you a carrot, an egg, or a coffee bean?"

The story urges us to reflect deeply on how we handle adversity. Are we like the carrot, initially strong but prone to losing our strength when faced with hardships? Are we like the egg, starting with a soft heart but becoming hardened by the trials we endure? Or are we like the coffee bean, capable of transforming even the most challenging situations into something better?

The coffee bean, in particular, teaches us a profound lesson. It changes the very circumstance that brings it pain. When life's waters boil around us, do we rise to the occasion and transform adversity into an opportunity for growth and positive change? Do we elevate ourselves to another level when times are at their toughest?

In closing, this story reminds us that the path to resilience is not always straightforward. It asks us to ponder our responses to adversity, to consider whether we wilt like carrots, harden like eggs, or transform like coffee beans. May you find enough happiness to stay sweet, enough trials to grow strong, enough sorrow to remain human, and enough hope to stay happy.

The brightest future can be built upon a forgotten past, but only if we let go of our past failures and heartaches.

9

Make Your Own Action Plan

"Healing may not be so much about getting better, as about letting go of everything that isn't you–all of the expectations, all of the beliefs–and becoming who you are."

— Rachel Naomi Remen

Throughout this book, we've explored various facets of mental health recovery, from understanding grief and depression to cultivating resilience and self-acceptance. Now, it's time to put these insights into action, tailored to your unique needs and aspirations.

In this ninth chapter, we'll embark on a purely practical stage. We'll work together to create a roadmap that aligns with your personal goals, values, and circumstances. Always mind that healing is a dynamic process, and your path may look very different from anyone else's. That's why your personalized action plan is so crucial—it's a compass guiding you toward a future filled with resilience, well-being, and authentic self-discovery. You've explored the depths of grief, delved into the intricacies of depression, and learned to cultivate resilience and self-acceptance. These insights are your tools, and now it's time to put them to use.

Let's begin by exploring the essential components of your action plan, and then we'll delve into the practical steps to make it a reality.

We will name this program our Healing Action Plan (HAP): a dynamic tool designed to help you navigate the stages of healing described in this book. It's an opportunity to turn your newfound knowledge into tangible steps toward a future marked by emotional well-being and personal growth.

Step 1: Reflect on your journey

- Take a moment to revisit the key takeaways from each chapter. What resonated with you the most? What concepts or strategies stood out as particularly relevant to your situation?

- Recognize how far you've come on your healing journey. Celebrate your achievements, no matter how small they may seem, by small but meaningful actions like preparing a special meal for you, taking a day off from responsibilities, booking a spa day, or taking a relaxing bath listening to music and smelling essential oils.

- Be honest with yourself about the challenges you've encountered. Identifying these obstacles is the first step in overcoming them.

Step 2: Aligning your plan with the stages of healing

Now, let's align your HAP with the stages of healing discussed in this book. Remember that your journey might not follow a linear path; that's perfectly okay. The key is to adapt and grow as you progress.

Stage 1: Understanding pain

- What specific aspects of your grief do you want to explore further? Are there unresolved emotions or memories you need to confront?

- List strategies you've learned for understanding and processing your grief, such as journaling or seeking support from others.

Stage 2: Navigating depression

- What changes do you want to make in your daily life to better manage depressive symptoms? What coping strategies will you implement?

- Detail the strategies you've found most effective for navigating depression, such as mindfulness or engaging in activities that boost your mood like riding a bike, playing an instrument, going for a walk with your dog, or simply lying down in the grass to read a book.

Stage 3: Cultivating resilience and self-acceptance

- How will you continue to build your resilience? What practices will help you maintain self-acceptance?

- Include strategies that have empowered you to cultivate resilience and embrace self-acceptance.

Step 3: Action steps

- For each goal you've set in alignment with the stages of healing, break it down into actionable steps. What can you do today, this week, or this month to move closer to your goals?

- Imagine yourself successfully achieving these goals. How would your life be different? Visualization can be a powerful motivator.

Step 4: Monitoring and adjusting

- Establish milestones to track your progress. Celebrate your achievements along the way.

- Regularly assess your action plan's effectiveness. If something isn't working, don't hesitate to adjust your strategies.

Step 5: Resources and support

- Ensure you have a support network in place, whether it's friends, family, or support groups. Share your action plan with them so they can offer encouragement and accountability.

HAPs are an essential part of any healing process. Each person has unique needs, traits, and experiences on the table. That is why it's so important to design a plan that aligns with the specific circumstances of the person.

So, what's the proper process to design your HAP? Before diving into the action plan, a comprehensive initial assessment must be conducted, where the individual's story, struggles, and goals are put on the table. Then, it is time to discuss their strengths, past experiences, and the challenges they're facing. This initial assessment forms the foundation upon which they build the personalized plan.

Then, specific and achievable goals are set, resonating with the person's unique situation. For example, if someone is struggling with depression, their goals might include improving sleep quality, practicing self-compassion, and seeking professional therapy.

Certainly, this plan is not static. It evolves as the person's situation does. If a strategy isn't yielding the expected results, it may be necessary to redesign and readapt it.

This is the path to ensure the plan takes a holistic approach, addressing mental, emotional, and physical well-being. If someone's depression is impacting their physical health, they might integrate exercise routines or nutritional guidance into the plan, for example.

It's a good idea to have regular check-ins scheduled to monitor progress and celebrate successes. These junctures are opportunities to evaluate what's working and what isn't, allowing adjustments to the plan accordingly. You can take a day per week to reflect on how your process is going, how well the employed strategies so far are working, and how you feel compared to the last check-in.

For sure, two central themes in these action plans must be the extensively discussed notions of self-compassion and resilience. The focus is on fostering self-compassion as a means of embracing imperfections and setbacks while simultaneously cultivating resilience to navigate challenges and setbacks. Since progress may not be linear most of the time, it's important to be ready to face knocks and overcome them.

This plan is a testament to your commitment to your well-being. It's a living document that can evolve with you as you continue to grow. By breaking your journey into manageable steps, you're taking ownership of your healing and personal growth. You've got this; those who love you, and I, are here to support you every step of the way.

10

Extra Exercises to Recover From Abandonment

"The greatest healing therapy is friendship and love."

— Hubert H. Humphrey

In my earlier years, life unfolded in a series of unexpected twists and turns. It seemed as if each road I traveled led to a new set of hurdles. But there was one pivotal moment that stands out, a moment that would alter the course of my life forever—my own encounter with abandonment.

This chapter of my life was marked by a fierce sea of emotions. Feelings of isolation, confusion, and a deep sense of loss threatened to overwhelm me. It was a time when I could have chosen to be a victim of my circumstances, to let the waves of despair swallow me whole. But I refused to be defeated.

Instead, I had to find self-discovery to find healing. It was a path that led me to explore the complex workings of the human mind and the sophistication of our emotional landscapes. I read voraciously, seeking understanding in the wisdom of psychology's great thinkers. I engaged in therapy, not as a patient, but as a student, learning the intricacies of the therapeutic process firsthand.

Through this introspection and self-study, a profound realization washed over me. I understood that healing wasn't just about mending wounds; it was about transforming pain into strength, vulnerability into resilience, and despair into hope. I then knew that my purpose in life was to guide others on this pathway.

Becoming a psychologist wasn't merely a career choice; it was a calling; the convergence of my personal experiences, my unwavering belief in the indomitable human spirit, and the burning desire to illuminate the path of healing for others who faced their trials.

And so, with this final chapter, we come full circle. Here, I'll share with you extra exercises and strategies to assist in your recovery from abandonment. It's a culmination of the knowledge, insights, and action plans we've developed throughout this book.

I invite you to walk alongside me not just as a reader but as a fellow traveler on the winding road of life. Within these pages, you'll find the tools to recover from abandonment and emerge from the shadows of anguish stronger than ever.

Start Writing

While the previous chapters have laid the foundation, these additional exercises will also be powerful tools to boost your healing process:

- Start by understanding that forgiveness isn't about excusing the actions of others but about liberating yourself from the emotional burden they may have caused. Consider writing letters of forgiveness to those who may have abandoned or hurt you. Explore how forgiveness can be a pivotal step toward acceptance, freeing you from the weight of resentment.

- Keep a reflective journal to identify abandonment triggers and the thought patterns that accompany them.

- Establish a gratitude journal to balance the pain of abandonment with moments of appreciation. Every day, jot down three things you are thankful for. This simple practice can gradually shift your focus from loss to abundance.

Prompts serve as invaluable tools for self-reflection and emotional processing. Consider the following prompts to guide your abandonment recovery journey:

- Set aside time each week to answer three fundamental questions: *What insights have I gained about myself this week? What progress have I made in my healing journey? How can I show more self-compassion in the coming week?* Over time, this practice allows you to witness your growth and evolution.

- Dive deep into your fears and insecurities connected to abandonment. Conversely, reflect on your strengths and sources of resilience that have carried you through challenging times. This exercise can help you uncover the inner resources that empower your healing.

- Consider writing letters to your younger self or to people who played significant roles in your abandonment experiences. These letters can provide a sense of closure, forgiveness, and healing. Use this space to express your feelings authentically and honestly. Let me give you an example:

Dear [Name of the person who abandoned you],

I hope this letter finds you well. It's been a long time since we last communicated, and there are many thoughts and feelings that I've carried with me over the years. I want to take this opportunity to share them with you, not to blame or accuse, but to find a sense of closure and healing.

I remember the day you left, and it left a lasting impact on me. As a child, I didn't fully understand why you had to go, and it created a void in my life. I felt abandoned, confused, and hurt. I often wondered if I had done something wrong to make you leave.

Over the years, I've come to realize that everyone has their own journey and struggles. I've tried to understand your perspective and the reasons behind your decisions. While I may never fully comprehend everything, I want you to know that I'm willing to let go of the anger and resentment that I've carried for so long.

Writing this letter is a way for me to release the pain I've held onto. I no longer want to define my life by the abandonment I experienced as a child. Instead, I want to find a path to healing and forgiveness.

I hope that you are finding your own path in life, one that brings you happiness and fulfillment. We all make choices that we later regret, and I understand that now. Holding onto this anger only hurts me, not you.

In writing this letter, I am choosing to forgive and move forward with my life. I want to heal the wounds of the past and create a brighter future for myself. I hope that you can find forgiveness in your heart as well, not just for me but for yourself.

Thank you for taking the time to read this letter. I wish you well on your journey, wherever it may lead.

Sincerely,

Myself.

Meditation and Recovery

Meditation can be a transformative practice to enhance emotional well-being during abandonment recovery. Explore these two guided meditations tailored to your journey:

- **Self-compassion meditation:** Find a quiet, comfortable space. Close your eyes and take deep breaths. Inhale self-compassion and exhale self-judgment. Repeat positive affirmations such as "I am deserving of love and acceptance." Visualize a warm, compassionate light enveloping you, soothing emotional wounds, and fostering self-compassion.

- **Self-forgiveness meditation:** Begin by acknowledging any guilt or self-blame you may carry from past experiences. As you breathe deeply, visualize forgiving yourself for perceived shortcomings or mistakes. Imagine a sense of forgiveness washing over you, releasing self-criticism and negativity.

To effectively incorporate these exercises into your daily life and navigate your abandonment recovery journey, consider these practical action steps:

- **Routine is key:** Allocate a specific time each day for self-reflection, emotional exercises, and meditation. Consistency is the bedrock of meaningful progress in abandonment recovery.

- **Set achievable goals:** Define realistic goals for your

journey. Perhaps you aim to forgive one person who has hurt you, or to identify and challenge one negative thought pattern every week. Realistic goals ensure steady progress.

- **Dedicate a journal:** Create a dedicated journal for your abandonment recovery journey. Use it to document your responses to prompts, track your progress, and authentically express your emotions.

Learn Your Attachment Style

Another important notion that I consider worth mentioning is attachment styles. These are ingrained patterns of emotional and behavioral responses that develop early in life, primarily during infancy and childhood, based on our interactions with our primary caregivers, usually parents or guardians. These prints profoundly influence how we perceive ourselves, how we relate to others, and how we navigate our emotions and relationships throughout our lives (Benoit, 2004).

These attachment styles are like emotional blueprints that guide our responses to various situations, especially in the context of close relationships. They encircle our beliefs about ourselves, our expectations of others, and our strategies for seeking comfort and security.

Here are the four primary attachment styles:

- **Secure attachment:** Individuals with a secure attachment style typically had caregivers who were responsive and consistently met their emotional and physical needs as children. As a result, they tend to have a positive view of themselves and others. They feel comfortable with emotional intimacy, can express their feelings openly, and believe they are deserving of love and support. Securely attached individuals tend to build healthy, trusting relationships based on mutual respect and understanding.

- **Anxious attachment:** People with an anxious attachment style often experience inconsistent caregiving during their early years. They may have had caregivers who were sometimes attentive and loving but at other times, distant or neglectful. Consequently, they tend to fear rejection and abandonment and may be preoccupied with their relationships. Individuals in such circumstances tend to continuously require affirmation and validation from their significant others, potentially developing a heightened reliance on them for emotional stability and contentment (Benoit, 2004).

- **Avoidant attachment:** Those with an avoidant attachment style typically had caregivers who emphasized independence and self-sufficiency. Their emotional needs may not have been consistently met in childhood, leading them to develop self-reliance as a coping strategy. As adults, they may find it challenging to open up emotionally or rely on others for support. They often prioritize self-sufficiency and may appear emotionally distant or dismissive of emotional intimacy.

- **Disorganized attachment:** This attachment style arises from inconsistent or traumatic caregiving experiences during childhood. Individuals with a disorganized attachment style often have caregivers who are unpredictable or even abusive. As a result, they may struggle with emotional regulation and may exhibit unpredictable behaviors in their adult relationships. This style combines elements of anxious and avoidant behaviors and can lead to significant challenges in forming healthy, stable relationships.

Here are some recommendations you can apply that will help you identify your attachment style and tailor your approach accordingly:

- **Engage in reflection:** Take time for deep self-reflection. Think about your past and your early relationships, especially with your primary caregivers. Consider how they responded to your emotional needs and how you felt in those relationships, since these early experiences significantly shape our way of building relationships.

- **Observe your relationship patterns:** Pay attention to your current relationships, both romantic and non-romantic. Notice how you respond to intimacy, emotional expression, and conflict. Do you tend to seek reassurance from others? Do you find it challenging to open up emotionally? Are you comfortable with vulnerability, or do you often withdraw?

- **Assess your emotional responses:** Explore your emotional responses in different situations. How do you react when you feel rejected or abandoned? Do you become anxious, clingy, or overwhelmed, or do you tend to distance yourself and become emotionally detached? Understanding your emotional reactions can provide valuable insights into your attachment style.

Once you've identified your attachment style, you can adapt your approach to foster recovery and healing:

- If you have a **secure attachment** style, you likely have a strong foundation for emotional well-being. Focus on maintaining and nurturing your healthy relationships. Use your secure base to explore and address abandonment issues with confidence.

- On the other hand, if you consider yourself to have an **anxious attachment** style, work on building self-esteem and self-reliance. Seek support to address underlying abandonment-related fears and develop strategies to manage anxiety in relationships.

- For those with an **avoidant attachment** style, challenge your avoidance of emotional intimacy. Practice opening up to trusted individuals and seek therapy to explore and heal past wounds that may be contributing to your avoidant tendencies.

- People with a **disorganized attachment** style can opt for activities like prompt journals, self-reflection, and mindfulness. This is often the most challenging attachment style, and it's systematically observed in the clinical field every day. That's why professional guidance may particularly benefit people with this attachment style—especially trauma-informed therapy (Wei, 2008).

These attachment styles are not fixed or mutually exclusive. They are mere frameworks that analysts have created in order to generalize and develop specific solutions for each one. Yet, through consistent internal work, you can adapt these categories and thus, strategies, to your specific situation.

Ready to explore your attachment style in depth? Immerse yourself in the insights and strategies of one of my other books, ***"Overcoming Anxious Attachment****: Your 3-step Healing Journey to Emotional Freedom, Finding Love and Security, and Building Healthy Relationships."*

Seek Help

Finally, but no less important: Seek help. I must insist on this. It's incredible how many people I see in my office every week who tell me I'm the first person they openly talk about their struggles with.

The power of companionship, love, and support is immeasurable. If you find yourself thinking that nobody cares about you, remember that reaching out is a vital step in your healing journey. It might be challenging, but even small steps can make a difference. Consider exploring support groups, online communities, or helplines. Sometimes, connecting with understanding individuals who have experienced similar struggles can be a powerful source of comfort and healing. And don't hesitate to lean on the pillars of your support system when you're ready. Healing often thrives in the presence of understanding friends, empathetic family members, or a skilled therapist.

Your determination and will to live a better life, both for yourself and for the people you cherish, are your driving forces. You possess the resilience to rebuild, even in the face of abandonment's profound pain. Every exercise, every journal entry, every moment of meditation, and every action step you take is a testament to your courage and strength.

Abandonment may have left its mark, but it doesn't define your destiny. You have the power to emerge from this journey not as a victim, but as a survivor—a survivor who's grown wiser, more compassionate, and deeply connected to your own authenticity.

You are now equipped with the tools to rebuild, to heal, and to thrive yourself. Your expedition of healing and recovery continues beyond these pages, and I have unwavering faith in your ability to create a life that reflects your true essence.

Bonus: Your Free Gifts

You've likely come across the bonuses several times throughout the book. If you want more tools and tips, these are your go-to guides. I'm offering these bonuses exclusively to my readers as a special thank you. Below, I've listed them once more, giving you one last opportunity to download them for free:

1. **The Self-Compassion Workbook** – A practical guide filled with exercises, reflections, and meditations to help you nurture self-compassion as a cornerstone of healing and recovery. (*$12.99*)
2. **Your Mood Tracker** – A simple yet effective tool to help you monitor your emotions, recognize patterns, and take control of your mental well-being. (*$11.99*)
3. **30-Day Self-Care Challenge** – A month-long challenge featuring daily self-care prompts and activities to help you build sustainable habits for balance and wellness. (*$16.99*)
4. **22 CBT Worksheets** – Evidence-based cognitive-behavioral therapy exercises designed to help you challenge negative thoughts and foster a more positive mindset. (*19.95*)
5. **80 Grief, Loss, and Heartbreak Affirmation Cards** – A collection of powerful affirmations to guide you through healing and provide support during moments of emotional pain and loss. (*24.99*)

Total Cost for You Today / ~~$86,91~~ - FREE!

To receive these exclusive **bonuses** immediately, scan the QR code now or directly go to: https://booksforbetterlife.com/abandonment-recovery

Conclusion

"Being challenged in life is inevitable, being defeated is optional."

— Roger Crawford

Throughout these pages, we've delved into the depths of abandonment, loss, grief, and acceptance, among other experiences and skills, peering into the intricate facets of these emotions to better understand their impact on our lives. We've explored the therapeutic approaches grounded in science, embracing the evidence-based methods that form the bedrock of emotional healing. We've ventured into the transformative power of acceptance, nurturing self-love and self-acceptance, and crafting a holistic action plan tailored to your unique journey. We've even delved into the nuanced realm of abandonment recovery, providing exercises, prompts, meditations, and action steps to guide you toward profound healing.

Each chapter has been a stepping stone on your path, offering insights and tools to empower you in your healing journey. But remember, you hold the key to your own transformation. As you navigate the complexities of emotional healing, use the knowledge you've acquired here as a compass, guiding you

CONCLUSION

through the darkest of storms. These pages have been a map, and now it's time for you to chart your own course.

In a world awash with information, it's crucial to approach emotional healing with discernment and an unwavering commitment to evidence-based practices. Your healing journey deserves nothing less.

As you close this chapter in your life, I invite you to commit wholeheartedly to your healing experience. Reach out to those who love and support you. Seek the guidance of skilled professionals when needed. Forge connections with kindred spirits who are on similar paths. Together, we create a network of strength, compassion, and resilience that can weather any storm.

Embrace the transformation that lies ahead. It won't always be easy, but it will be worth it. Healing is not a linear path—it's a mosaic of experiences, emotions, and growth. Embrace the mosaic and find beauty in its complexity.

As we part ways on this page, know that I am deeply grateful to have shared this journey with you. Your commitment to healing is not only a testament to your strength but also a gift to those who are fortunate enough to know you. As you step into the next chapter of your life, I wish you a life filled with joy, fulfillment, and boundless love.

Thank you for being a part of this transformative journey. May your days be filled with peace, your heart with love, and your spirit with unbreakable resilience.

With profound respect and heartfelt gratitude,

Cher Hampton.

References

Angelou, M. (1999). *I know why the caged bird sings*. Oxford University Press.

Benoit, D. (2004). Infant-parent attachment: Definition, types, antecedents, measurement and outcome. *Paediatrics & Child Health*, *9*(8), 541–545. https://doi.org/10.1093/pch/9.8.541

Biography. (2021, March 31). *Audrey Hepburn: Movies, quotes & death*. https://www.biography.com/actors/audrey-hepburn

Blackburn, T. P. (2019). Depressive disorders: Treatment failures and poor prognosis over the last 50 years. *Pharmacology Research & Perspectives*, *7*(3), Article e00472. https://doi.org/10.1002/prp2.472

Bomyea, J., Ball, T. M., Simmons, A. N., Campbell-Sills, L., Paulus, M. P., & Stein, M. B. (2020). Change in neural response during emotion regulation is associated with symptom reduction in cognitive behavioral therapy for anxiety disorders. *Journal of Affective Disorders*, *271*, 207–214. https://doi.org/10.1016/j.jad.2020.04.001

Bowlby, J. (1969). *Attachment and loss* (Vol. 1). Pimlico.

Charney, D. S. (2003). The psychobiology of resilience and vulnerability to anxiety disorders: Implications for prevention and treatment. *Dialogues in Clinical Neuroscience, 5*(3), 207–221. https://doi.org/10.31887/dcns.2003.5.3/dcharney

Davydov, D. M., Zech, E., & Luminet, O. (2011). Affective context of sadness and physiological response patterns. *Journal of Psychophysiology, 25*(2), 67–80. https://doi.org/10.1027/026 9-8803/a000031

Dettori, M., Azara, A., Loria, E., Piana, A., Masia, M., Palmieri, A., Cossu, A., & Castiglia, P. (2019). Population distrust of drinking water safety. Community outrage analysis, prediction and management. *International Journal of Environmental Research and Public Health, 16*(6), 1004. https://doi.org/10.3390/ijerph1 6061004

DiBartolo, P. M., Frost, R. O., Chang, P., LaSota, M., & Grills, A. E. (2004). Shedding light on the relationship between personal standards and psychopathology: The case for contingent self-worth. *Journal of Rational-Emotive & Cognitive-Behavior Therapy, 22*(4), 237–250. https://doi.org/10.1023/b:jore.0000 047310.94044.ac

Encyclopædia Britannica. (n.d.). *Waka: Japanese poetry.* https://www.britannica.com/art/waka-Japanese-poetry

Faye, U. (2021). *Sutras of the heart.* Self-published.

Fritscher, L. (2019). *How a fear of intimacy can cause you to avoid or sabotage relationships.* Verywell Mind. https://www.verywell

mind.com/fear-of-intimacy-2671818

Dostoevsky, F. (2022). *The dream of a ridiculous man*. Lindhardt Og Ringhof.

Garner, B., Phassouliotis, C., Phillips, L. J., Markulev, C., Butselaar, F., Bendall, S., Yun, Y., & McGorry, P. D. (2011). Cortisol and dehydroepiandrosterone-sulfate levels correlate with symptom severity in first-episode psychosis. *Journal of Psychiatric Research*, *45*(2), 249–255. https://doi.org/10.1016/j.jpsychires.2010.06.008

Goodreads. (n.d.). *A quote by Rumi*. https://www.goodreads.com/quotes/103315-the-wound-is-the-place-where-the-light-enters-you

Greden, J. (2003). Physical symptoms of depression. *J Clin Psychiatry*, *64*(7).

Hofmann, S. G., Asnaani, A., Vonk, I. J. J., Sawyer, A. T., & Fang, A. (2012). The efficacy of cognitive behavioral therapy: A review of meta-analyses. *Cognitive Therapy and Research*, *36*(5), 427–440. https://doi.org/10.1007/s10608-012-9476-1

Hofmann, S. G., Sawyer, A. T., Witt, A. A., & Oh, D. (2010). The effect of mindfulness-based therapy on anxiety and depression: A meta-analytic review. *Journal of Consulting and Clinical Psychology*, *78*(2), 169–183. https://doi.org/10.1037/a0018555

Hölzel, B. K., Carmody, J., Vangel, M., Congleton, C., Yerramsetti, S. M., Gard, T., & Lazar, S. W. (2011). Mindfulness practice leads to increases in regional brain gray matter density. *Psychiatry Research: Neuroimaging, 191*(1), 36–43. https://doi.org/10.1016/j.pscychresns.2010.08.006

Jayawickreme, E., & Blackie, L. E. R. (2014). Post-traumatic growth as positive personality change: Evidence, controversies and future directions. *European Journal of Personality, 28*(4), 312–331. https://doi.org/10.1002/per.1963

Jhonson, D. (2022, February 11). *The science of sadness*. Cosmosmagazine.com. https://cosmosmagazine.com/health/body-and-mind/the-science-of-sadness/

Knaak, S., Mantler, E., & Szeto, A. (2017). Mental illness-related stigma in healthcare. *Healthcare Management Forum, 30*(2), 111–116. https://doi.org/10.1177/0840470416679413

Körner, A., Coroiu, A., Copeland, L., Gomez-Garibello, C., Albani, C., Zenger, M., & Brähler, E. (2015). The role of self-compassion in buffering symptoms of depression in the general population. *PLOS ONE, 10*(10), Article e0136598. https://doi.org/10.1371/journal.pone.0136598

Kramer, E. J., Kwong, K., Lee, E., & Chung, H. (2002). Cultural factors influencing the mental health of Asian Americans. *The Western Journal of Medicine, 176*(4), 227–231. https://www.ncbi.nlm.nih.gov/pmc/articles/PMC1071736/

Kringelbach, M. L., & Berridge, K. C. (2009). Towards a functional neuroanatomy of pleasure and happiness. *Trends in Cognitive Sciences, 13*(11), 479–487. https://doi.org/10.1016/j.t

ics.2009.08.006

Kübler-Ross, E., & Kessler, D. (2005). *On grief and grieving: Finding the meaning of grief through the five stages of loss.* Simon & Schuster.

Ma, X., Yue, Z.-Q., Gong, Z.-Q., Zhang, H., Duan, N.-Y., Shi, Y.-T., Wei, G.-X., & Li, Y.-F. (2017). The effect of diaphragmatic breathing on attention, negative affect and stress in healthy adults. *Frontiers in Psychology, 8*(874), 1–12. https://doi.org/10.3389/fpsyg.2017.00874

Merriam-Webster. (n.d.). Abandonment. In *Merriam-Webster.com dictionary.* Retrieved October 4, 2023, from https://www.merriam-webster.com/dictionary/abandonment

Monroe, S. M., Rohde, P., Seeley, J. R., & Lewinsohn, P. M. (1999). Life events and depression in adolescence: Relationship loss as a prospective risk factor for first onset of major depressive disorder. *Journal of Abnormal Psychology, 108*(4), 606–614. https://doi.org/10.1037/0021-843x.108.4.606

Naskar, A. (2023). *Yarasistan.* Self-published.

Niles, A. N., Haltom, K. E. B., Mulvenna, C. M., Lieberman, M. D., & Stanton, A. L. (2013). Randomized controlled trial of expressive writing for psychological and physical health: The moderating role of emotional expressivity. *Anxiety, Stress, & Coping, 27*(1), 1–17. https://doi.org/10.1080/10615806.2013.802308

O'Connor, M.-F. (2019). Grief: A brief history of research on how body, mind, and brain adapt. *Psychosomatic Medicine, 81*(8), 731–738. https://doi.org/10.1097/PSY.0000000000000717

O'Hara, M. (1989). Person-centered approach as conscientizacao: The works of Carl Rogers and Paulo Freire. *Journal of Humanistic Psychology, 29*(1), 11–35. https://doi.org/10.1177/0022167889291002

Pressman, S. D., Matthews, K. A., Cohen, S., Martire, L. M., Scheier, M., Baum, A., & Schulz, R. (2009). Association of enjoyable leisure activities with psychological and physical Well-Being. *Psychosomatic Medicine, 71*(7), 725–732. https://doi.org/10.1097/psy.0b013e3181ad7978

Rauwenhoff, J. C. C., Bol, Y., Peeters, F., van den Hout, A. J. H. C., Geusgens, C. A. V., & van Heugten, C. M. (2022). Acceptance and commitment therapy for individuals with depressive and anxiety symptoms following acquired brain injury: A non-concurrent multiple baseline design across four cases. *Neuropsychological Rehabilitation*, 1–31. https://doi.org/10.1080/09602011.2022.2053169

Sukhodolsky, D. G., Smith, S. D., McCauley, S. A., Ibrahim, K., & Piasecka, J. B. (2016). Behavioral interventions for anger, irritability, and aggression in children and adolescents. *Journal of Child and Adolescent Psychopharmacology, 26*(1), 58–64. https://doi.org/10.1089/cap.2015.0120

Tamam, S., & Ahmad, A. H. (2017). Love as a modulator of pain. *Malaysian Journal of Medical Sciences, 24*(3), 5–14. https://doi.o

rg/10.21315/mjms2017.24.3.2

Tang, Y.-Y., Hölzel, B. K., & Posner, M. I. (2015). The neuroscience of mindfulness meditation. *Nature Reviews Neuroscience*, *16*(4), 213–225. https://doi.org/10.1038/nrn3916

Trivedi, M. H. (2004). The link between depression and physical symptoms. *Primary Care Companion to the Journal of Clinical Psychiatry*, *6*(Suppl 1), 12–16. https://www.ncbi.nlm.nih.gov/pmc/articles/PMC486942/

Tyrrell, P., Harberger, S., Schoo, C., & Siddiqui, W. (2023, February 26). Kubler-Ross stages of dying and subsequent models of grief. In *StatPearls [Internet]*. StatPearls Publishing.

Umberson, D., & Karas Montez, J. (2010). Social relationships and health: A flashpoint for health policy. *Journal of Health and Social Behavior*, *51*(1), 54–66. https://doi.org/10.1177/0022146510383501

The University of Texas at Austin. (n.d.). A carrot, an egg, and a cup of coffee: Transforming lives through resilience education. http://sites.edb.utexas.edu/resilienceeducation/inspiring-stories/a-carrot-an-egg-and-a-cup-of-coffee/

Wei, M. (2008, October 15). *The implications of attachment theory in counseling and psychotherapy | Society for the advancement of psychotherapy*. Society for the Advancement of Psychotherapy. https://societyforpsychotherapy.org/the-implications-of-attachment-theory-in-counseling-and-psychotherapy/

World Health Organization. (2023, March 31). *Depression*. https://www.who.int/news-room/fact-sheets/detail/depression

Zhang, X., Yue, H., Sun, J., Liu, M., Li, C., & Bao, H. (2022). Regulatory emotional self-efficacy and psychological distress among medical students: Multiple mediating roles of interpersonal adaptation and self-acceptance. *BMC Medical Education, 22*(1). https://doi.org/10.1186/s12909-022-03338-2

Printed in Dunstable, United Kingdom